The Future
of GOD

Carl E. Braaten

The Revolutionary
Dynamics of
Hope

The Future
of GOD

Harper & Row, Publishers
New York, Evanston, and London

FIRST EDITION

LIBRARY OF CONGRESS CATALOG CARD NUMBER: 69-17024

To LaVonne

Contents

Preface

In the long run it may become evident that radical theology has been having a cathartic effect on the church and its theology. The "death of God" phase may have helped to force theology to find a new beginning. I am a partisan in this quest for a new way to start theology. Therefore, while I am unable to count myself, and few others would wish to number me, among the radical theologians, I feel myself closer to them than this book, or any of my other writings, can adequately indicate. Their questions are always in my mind. Their answers are always challenging those I prefer. I share with them some of the shock at witnessing the collapse of the going systems. Whether one cut his theological eyeteeth more on Barth, Bultmann, or Tillich, the feeling is quite general that we can hardly go on the way we have been going. But how do we begin again? Where do we go from here?

This book on the concept of the future works in alliance with a new movement in modern theology which grasps the gravity of the issues which confront the church and its theology today. The new place to start in theology is at the end—eschatology. The rediscovery of the role of eschatology in the preaching of Jesus and of early Christianity has been one of the most important events of recent theological history. The findings of biblical theologians, however, have not always been taken seriously by systematic theologians. The main response of systematic theology to the rediscovery of eschatology has been so to redefine the eschatology in question that it loses its futurity. Eschatology has been predominantly understood as the dimension of the eternal shining through the temporal in rather Platonic fashion. This is true not only of the Continentals who have operated under some version of dialectical or existentialist theology but also of the Anglo-Saxons who, following C. H. Dodd, have accepted some form of realized eschatology. Both in exegetical and in systematic circles the dimension of the future in biblical eschatology has been a source of embarrassment. This horror of the future is perhaps best understood as a sign of the degree to which modern theology as a function of the church has succumbed to the establishmentarian mentality that has crippled the Christian movement in modern times, and set it in opposition to the revolutionary forces at work to change the world. Revolutionary thinking is always oriented to the future; it does not accept the past or the status quo as the picture of the "homeland" and "happy days" which all men seek in one way or another. It has been good form for future-less Christians to deride utopianism. Little did they realize—or did they—that in chucking utopianism altogether they lost their own eschatology which looks to the future of God's final and fulfilling coming. It is this loss of eschatology which has precipitated that mood in theology which feels it has lost God. Hope-lessness is God-lessness, because both are future-lessness.

Hope is a word whose correlate is the future. As a questioning being, man is oriented in hope toward the future. The categories of "hope" and "future" are crucial in the new theology which begins with eschatology. For this reason it is variously referred to as a "theology of hope" or a "theology of the future," but sometimes also as a "theology of promise" or a "theology of revolution." What one cares to call it matters very little, except that every new movement finds its own slogans, its own alluring rhetoric. A theology that addresses the "whole man" should not be faulted for using rhetoric, provided that that does not blur the rationality of its vision. Especially when one's vision orients to the future, there is admittedly a need for reason to apply the breaks and to give an account of the logic of the language of hope that prospects the future. We do not claim to have offered more than a start toward such an account. But had we achieved even more, it would not be convincing enough to many of our contemporaries who conform to the image Herbert Marcuse has so skillfully drawn in his *One-Dimensional Man.*

"One-dimensional man" is given to a preference for ordinary language that deals with the ordinary world of "words and things." We have instead turned to extraordinary language, the visionary language of hope, the utopian language of revolutionaries, and the apocalyptic language of the future. This is language which transgresses against the ready-made world. It gives us some resources from which to contradict and violate the established universe of discourse. The aim of our interest in the extraordinary language of future-oriented thinkers is manifestly revolutionary. That is a Christian prejudice we share with the early Christians whose hope was pulled forward by the future of God's coming kingdom.

The story of the idea of the future in modern theology is one that unfolds in at least three steps. First, the giants of the older generation—Barth, Bultmann, and Tillich—let the dimension of the future slip into an eternal present, with the result that the transcendence of God could only be viewed in vertical terms as "above us" or, as the case may be, "below us." Second, the "death of God" stage in theology, following so quickly on the heels of the older generation of dialectical theologians, was no accident. The "God above us" died as the retribution exacted from theology for the sterility of its future-less eschatology. We are now in a third stage that began with theologians like Pannenberg and Moltmann who seized upon the occasion to take up the theme of eschatology as a new point of departure for a total recasting of the Christian message. A number of factors contributed to the ripening of the moment—the futurological tendencies in modern culture, the stimulus of Ernst Bloch's philosophy of hope, the rediscovery of apocalypticism in earliest Christian circles and in the historical Jesus, besides the exposure of critical weaknesses within the reigning systems of theology.

This book is a sketch of a theology oriented to the future, set forth almost as a "little dogmatic." It presupposes the prior stages in the development of modern Protestant theology. I do not believe it is possible or desirable to try to make any headway without maintaining continuity with the immediately preceding theology. On the other hand, we must try to go further. We have concluded our study with an ethic of revolution. This is the timely upshot of a theology that lives from the revolution which the eschatological history of God has set in motion. This is the place to confess, at the same time, that this ethic of revolution is a meager affair when measured by the enormity of the perils and promises of our epoch. One author need not do everything; there are kindred spirits working with great energy on this problem. And one can always hope that time and circumstance will be found to work out the more functional implications for the church of a theology of revolution. What this must mean for preaching, for gathering in worship, for Christian education, for the ministry of healing, for mission to non-Christians, for social and political action, is something which only a team of minds will be able to grasp. Too often in the church we are given today the functional implications of yesterday's theology for tomorrow's world. And that is why theological education languishes on the brink of boredom for so many students.

This book could not have been written without the intellectual stimulus I have received from Wolfhart Pannenberg. The writings of Jürgen Moltmann have also had a considerable influence on my thinking. The footnotes tell the degree of my indebtedness to them. What they do not tell, however, is the encouragement and reinforcements I received through countless conversations during my sabbatical year in Oxford with my friend Robert William Jenson, whose thought, to my surprise and joy, was converging on the same path as my own, his more from a Barthian, mine more from a Tillichian, angle. The unusual luxury of having a whole year's time off to write was made possible by the generous sabbatical program of the Lutheran School of Theology at Chicago and also by the award of a Fellowship of the John Simon Guggenheim Memorial Foundation. I have dedicated this book to my wife, LaVonne, who will understand why I do not repeat the needless sorts of things which authors are wont to say in prefaces about their wives.

Carl E. Braaten

Hyde Park, Chicago
January, 1969

The Future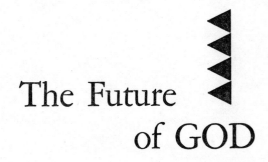
of GOD

INTRODUCTION

The Horizon
of the Future

1. DOING THEOLOGY AS ESCHATOLOGY

The aim of this book is to explore the revolutionary potential of the Christian idea of the future. Our concern is for the future of the Christian faith, but in a more basic sense it is quite simply for the future of mankind. Since a Christian is first of all a human being, the future for which he hopes must coincide with the future which he holds out for the whole of mankind. That future we call "God." The Christian faith is wholly oriented to God as the power of the future which arrived in Jesus of Nazareth under the signs of promise and hope.

The distance between biblical revelation and contemporary experience is being keenly felt today. The Bible belongs to a past world-view and makes little contact with the present situation of modern man. All our talk about hermeneutics today is a telltale sign of our difficulty. The thesis of this study is that the hermeneutical gap between the Bible and modern culture can be narrowed only within the horizon of the future common to both.

What is that horizon? That is the eschatological horizon of God's future which appeared in the Christ-happening. It is a future which in coming to pass in the openness of world history is never past because it continues to be the future of God out in front of the world in its present form. This futurist perspective may open up a hermeneutical way which finds border crossings between the eschatological horizon of the Bible and the orientation of our secular culture toward the open future. The way ahead is perhaps through a new coalition of theology with a philosophy of hope, of biblical apocalyptic eschatology with modern secular futurology.

The starting point of Christian theology is not at the beginning but at the end. What Ernst Bloch, the Marxist philosopher, puts forth as an ontological assertion we therefore adopt as our theological slogan: "The real genesis is not at the beginning, but at the end."[1] Eschatology, not archaeology or protology, is the source of light and life. The past and present are illuminated by the light that dawns in the morning of God's future. The Christian faith originally began from the power of God's creative eschaton. His eschatological word became flesh; revelation became history; the end of God's way with man was attained in a preliminary way through Jesus' resurrection unto new life; the last judgment of God is proleptically actualized even now through his justification of the godless by sheer grace. The eschatological orientation of Christian existence looks to the future as the decisive mode of time. The categories of hope and futurity are at the core of Christian faith. An impressive chorus of voices can be heard today in support of this claim. "Hope was the original impulse of theology,"[2] says Ernst Benz. Jürgen Moltmann states, "There is therefore only one real problem in Christian theology, which its own object forces upon it and which it in turn forces on mankind and on human thought: the problem of the future."[3] Gerhard Sauter wrote his massive *Habilitationsschrift* on the theme of the future in contemporary theology and philosophy.[4] In a similar vein Harvey Cox asserts, "The only future that theology has, one might say, is to become the theology of the future."[5] But it was the theology of Wolfhart Pannenberg that made the initial breakthrough to the triumph of the future as the controlling thematic in theology. His idea of the eschatological future is the key to his theology of universal history. Meanwhile, this futurist approach is making headway among Roman Catholic theologians, for example, Johannes Metz, Karl Rahner, and E. Schillebeeckx. Metz lays down a challenge to Catholic theology which could have effects far outreaching anything imagined at Vatican II. Doing theology within the horizon of the future, he says, "reveals the world as history, history as final history, faith as hope and theology as eschatology."[6]

The idea of doing theology as eschatology is not new; it has a familiar enough ring. From the very start the dialectical theologians, Barth and company, insisted that "Christianity that is not entirely and altogether eschatology has entirely and altogether nothing to do with Christ."[7] They taught that eschatology is not the last-stage thing which traditional dogmatics confined to its concluding chapter. Instead, eschatology permeates the whole of Christian faith. It is the dimension of the eternal breaking in from above and touching the present moment. For the early Barth, as well as for the later Tillich, the eschatology of the eternal now was dominant. The universal relevance of eschatology was gained by a radical redefinition in which the horizon of the future disappeared into the eternal depths of the present moment. In the case of Barth the future was absorbed into the *nunc aeternitatis*, manifest in the incarnate Word. In Bultmann's case the future was finally subjectivized into the futuricity of existence in the immediate present. The eschatological future became an existential stance of openness to the world. The future as the front line of God's advancing kingdom which generates the expectancy of really new happenings in world history was not the focus of faith in the period of dialectical theology. Neither Barth's theology of the word nor Bultmann's theology of existence gave us an eschatology that incorporated the horizontal line of history that moves outward and forward. Theology was eschatological in terms of a vertical dialectic between eternity and time, from above to below, but at the price of the horizon of the future. The activation of eschatology without surrendering its futural aspect has remained an unsolved problem along the whole line of theology that runs from early dialectical theology to more recent existentialist and hermeneutical theology.

Every theologian knows today about Albert Schweitzer's rediscovery of apocalyptic eschatology in the preaching of Jesus. For Schweitzer it was precisely this apocalypticism which alienated Jesus from modern culture and kept him riveted to the world-view of the first century. Schweitzer doubted that one could get a contemporary Christ out of an apocalyptic Jesus. So he developed a mystical philosophy of life totally free of any of the eschatology that motivated Jesus. Schweitzer protested the unhistorical treatment of the Gospels by many of his contemporaries who distilled from them a christological ethic, leaving behind as of no account the eschatological christology that underlies it. This unhistorical tactic is being revived today. Jesus of Nazareth is lifted out of the eschatological fog of his era and recommended to our world as "the man for others."[8] Or he is pictured as the man of faith, of freedom, of love, open to others, with an emulable style of existence. It is quite widely surmised that christology can build directly on Jesus' way with others, on an ethical substrate cleared by historical criticism of its apocalyptic overgrowth. The apocalyptic eschatology in the preaching of Jesus is then either traced—unsuccessfully—to later churchly redactions or dismissed—unscientifically—as of marginal significance in Jesus' own self-understanding. The impulse to modernize Jesus is still strong, and since modernity is supposedly open to ethics but allergic to apocalypticism, the pictures of Jesus are painted without restraint à la mode moderne. Jesus is now an existentialist gripped by the urgency of the moment, now a leader of a protest movement crusading for the underdogs. The neglect of Schweitzer's discovery leads to arbitrary and superficial treatments of the historical Jesus.

Doing theology as eschatology, beginning at the end, is a proposal to take seriously the apocalyptic character of the career and kerygma of Jesus. It is a proposal to seek the uniqueness of Jesus and his relevance to our time not outside of but within the horizon of the apocalyptic eschatology which Jesus shared with his age. The function of Jesus' proclamation of the imminent kingdom of God was not merely to announce that "time is of the essence" and "now is the hour of decision." It brings with it an understanding of reality as history, of man as hope, of revelation as promise, of the world in revolutionary change, and of God as the power of the future. Ernst Käsemann made an important step forward when he traced the beginnings of Christian theology to apocalypticism. In his words, "Apocalypticism was the mother of all Christian theology."[9] Käsemann, not unlike Schweitzer a half century before, called into question the attempts to build modern theology on an ethical or existentialist interpretation of the New Testament. Käsemann's target was not only Bultmann's existentialist kerygma but also the hermeneutical theology of Gerhard Ebeling and Ernst Fuchs.

The concept of kerygma in modern theology has functioned to designate that which faith and the present-day church may appropriate existentially from Jesus and early Christianity without ceasing to be wholly modern. It is the kerygma which constitutes the continuity between Jesus and the early church. It is the one thing needful. But what is it? If we ask this question of kerygmatic theology, we are usually told that the kerygma is indeed an eschatological phenomenon, but that is not to say that its content is shaped and structured by the apocalypticism of late-Jewish messianism. Now Käsemann has challenged this ploy with respect to the kerygma of early Christianity. There is no historically justifiable way of having recourse to the concept of an eschatological kerygma without taking along in the bargain the apocalyptic structure and content of early Christian preaching and teaching. Käsemann has shown that even Paul continued to be an apocalyptic thinker after he became an apostle of Christ.[10] But was it really so different with Jesus? Does it make sense to speak of Jesus' own kerygma as eschatological outside the framework of the apocalyptic view of history which he shared with his contemporaries? Have we not been operating theologically as if words like "kerygma" and "eschatological" possess a magic by which to break the spell of apocalypticism which afflicts the New Testament and keeps it in a world of its own? But these words have lost their magic due to more penetrating historical analysis. To the extent we inquire about the *content* of the kerygma, whether of Jesus or of Paul and the early church, and about the concept of eschatology, we find that we are pushed back into the tradition of apocalyptic thought which Johannes Weiss and Albert Schweitzer analyzed. We find that Jesus' own preaching of the kingdom of God carried unmistakable elements from the surrounding world of apocalyptic expectations. The breakdown of this distinction between "apocalyptic" and "eschatological" thought on which modern kerygmatic theology has staked its life presents exegesis and systematic theology with a dilemma. The more we stress the apocalyptic features the more it seems we increase our religious and cultural alienation from Jesus and primitive Christianity. The more the eschatological kerygma is apocalyptically constituted, the more it loses its immediate existential relevance. So it has seemed. And for this reason Käsemann's reopening of the apocalyptic thematic was vigorously opposed by G. Ebeling and E. Fuchs.[11] But others have confirmed and expanded his findings, so that modern exegesis and systematic theology can no longer ignore the constitutive significance of apocalypticism in Jesus' message of the kingdom of God and in the apostolic kerygma of the cross and resurrection.

The problem for a theology in close touch with exegesis is no longer how to get around the apocalypticism in Jesus. That way is barred by our historical knowledge. Rather, the challenge is to start with it and find within its horizon the decisive meaning of Jesus the Messiah for a contemporary understanding of the Christian faith. A truly contemporary understanding must take with equal seriousness the horizon of our own historical situation today. Wolfhart Pannenberg has defined the problem in terms of two different horizons of experience and thought, that of the Bible and that of modern culture.[12] How can these two horizons be connected, united, or merged? How can a Christian be both biblical and modern? How can the theologian be true to the distinctiveness of each of the horizons within which he must live and move? How can he serve two masters? For either he tends to hate the one and love the other, becoming a kind of biblical literalist, bound to the letter of Scripture as a book of legal doctrines, or he tends to be dedicated to the one and despise the other, a captive to the latest modernism with no transcendent vision from which to transgress against the status quo of his own time and place. The one makes an idol of the establishment of the past; the other bows down to the establishment of the present. Neither fundamentalism nor modernism solved the problem of the two horizons; neither offered an adequate hermeneutical bridge spanning the biblical message and modern culture.

2.   A NEW CORRELATION WITH FUTUROLOGY

What is needed today is a new correlation between the eschatological origins of Christian faith and the present revolutionary forces that seek to build a new and better future for mankind. Apocalyptic eschatology and secular futurology can be correlated and their horizons connected if they both orient upon a new horizon which includes them both, if they share the horizon of a common future that links the past to the present without sacrificing what is particular and valuable in each.[13] The horizon of the future can break the dualism of two rigidly self-sufficient horizons, that of the biblical records and that of the present age. The meaning of any historical event can be known only from its context. One must know the full context. However, the full context is unavailable, since history is still going on and has not come to an end. The future perspective must be included in any contextual interpretation of an event's meaning. The context of the past or of the present is not enough. Bultmann recognized that the dimension of the future is essential in historical interpretation. He wrote, "But what these events that can thus be dated *mean* as historical events cannot be definitively fixed. Hence one must say that a historical event is always first knowable for what it is—precisely as a historical event—*in the future*. And therefore one can also say that the future of a historical event belongs to that event."[14] Then he added, "It holds good that what a historical event means always first becomes clear *in the future*. It can definitely disclose itself only when history has come to an end."[15] In short, the meaning of history, past and present history and history as a whole, is linked to the horizon of the future. Bultmann discovered to our lasting gain that any serious wrestling with the hermeneutical problem opens up the question of a possible eschatological interpretation of history.

The historical study of the earliest Christian sources has focused our attention on the eschatological character of the message of Jesus and of the apostolic preaching of him as the Messiah. It is precisely by penetrating this message that the horizon of the future is suggested as one which can bridge the two horizons of the past and the present. Early Christianity proclaimed the eschatological message of the future of God and his advancing kingdom in Jesus as the goal of man's hope in every age. The deeper we delve into the heart of this eschatological message, the more it turns our hopes to the future of God. It opens up the horizon of the future of fulfillment, for the individual, for mankind as a whole, and the history of all reality. This message of the future is still a matter of hope and longing. Believers continue to pray each day, "Thy kingdom come." We look to the future for the source of power to change things as they are. The past has no power to change the present. That is not the function of the past, and to call upon it to serve the present in that way is a form both of slavery and of idolatry. Jesus made the claim that the quality of one's relation to the future of God's approaching kingdom was determined by one's relation to himself, but the futurity of this future was not exhausted in his earthly presence. There is no "realized eschatology" in the sense that the "not yet" of the future is wholly exhausted in the "already" of the present encounter with Jesus. The power of the future retained its own reality as future in the preaching of Jesus. In traditional Nicene categories we could say that when God becomes present in Jesus, he does not cease to be God. The incarnation is not a metamorphosis of one kind of being into another kind of being. In other words, in Jesus the future becomes present without being realized in such a way that it ceases to be still future. This is still—two thousand years later—a time of hope and growing expectation. The fulfillment is still outstanding, and when Christians forget this, they have the Jews to tell them, for they can recall that the promises that point to the coming of the messianic kingdom contain more than anyone has yet experienced in the world.

The horizon of the future that was opened up by the Christ-happening can embrace the horizon of the present age because it answers to the future-oriented structure of human existence and historical reality of which we moderns are particularly conscious. A theology that starts with eschatology must correlate with the conditions of modern experience and understanding. For this it requires an anthropology of hope, one that is oriented to the future. There is no doubt that the New Testament language of hope is oriented to the eschatological future of God. The question is whether that future can be envisioned today as the answer to man as such as a creature of hope. Is not the heart of man restless with hope until it finds its fulfillment in the future of God? Our theology is a wager that that is so.

Many theologies which have been passionately concerned to establish a foothold for Christian faith in modern secular thought have been most oblivious to its passion for the future. Not only has theology thereby been unfaithful to its own eschatological origins, but it has dampened the interest of men in earnest about the future of mankind. The Christian gospel can expect to get a hearing in modern culture only when it has some important news to bring about our human future, when it is really concerned about the world's tomorrows. If it has nothing to do with the future, it is properly and understandably dismissed as irrelevant. Christianity must learn again to take up the burdens of mankind for a better future. There is a much deserved sting in the eleventh and last of Karl Marx's *Theses on Feuerbach*: "The philosophers have only interpreted the world, in various ways; the point, however, is to *change* it."[16] Talk about changing the world implies that we assume responsibility for the future. Revolutionary change is the responsibility of eschatological hope.[17] This affirmation can be made without numbering a person among the activistic zealots whom Jesus called men of violence who would take the kingdom of God by force.[18] Christians who live by hope are en route with a passion for the future. This places them in tension with any mode of thinking which accepts this world as it is. The status quo is not what it is meant to be, no matter how good it seems. Eschatological imagination is filled with visions of new things. It inspires one to work to invalidate and subvert the facts, so that facts might become promissory signs of new reality breaking in from the future of God. Language has the function to call the new into being and to assign the past its place. The language of hope has a proleptic structure, anticipating the truth of reality that is not yet and that is awaited with eager longing.

Today's Christians find that they are not the only ones who dream dreams of a new and better future and are willing to work to usher it into existence. They find themselves mingling with other utopians, futurists, and revolutionaries who live toward the future of a new world. They are confronted by rival language systems of ideals, aspirations, and images which compete with the eschatological symbols of the Christian faith in mobilizing the loyalties of men. The truth and power of the Christian gospel must be made good within the public arena in which the future of man is being debated and decided. The eschatological message of Christianity has a point of contact today with those having a lively zest for the future. The future-less and hope-less outlook of a generation ago is no longer the dominant mood in our culture. There are surprising outbursts of interest in what is to come. The theological task is to take up, criticize, and advance the futurological tendencies in the modern world within the horizon of an eschatological concept of the future. Christian theology must reach back, with all possible energy of historical reason, to its own eschatological ground, and then search for the present signs of the kingdom of God *in, with,* and *under* the conditions of our secularized world. If the ultimate future of the world appeared in Jesus Christ, then our present history awaits its fulfillment from that same future. For this reason theology must take with utmost seriousness the future-oriented culture in which we live. Only in this way can there be a truly secular translation of the gospel. Christian hope toward the future of God's kingdom is based on its proleptic occurrence in Jesus of Nazareth. This hope must enter into dialogue with the sound or illusory hopes of secular futurologists and utopian humanists who do not name the name of the One whose Father has promised to await us as our Future. In view of the masses of Christians who no longer believe their own eschatology, the prospects for this dialogue with humanists and Marxists, with technocrats and scientists, may appear quite grim. The charter for this dialogue, however, has not been revoked: "Be ready always to give an answer to every man that asketh you a reason of the hope that is in you."[19]

Theological interest in the future intersects with secular futurology at the levels of both theory and praxis—of theory, because our view of the future in relation to past and present does affect our capacities for creative anticipation and action, and of praxis, because the human and social goals which technology should be made to serve are by no means self-evident. The machine is made for man and not man for the machine. What image of man and what picture of community guides our planning, fills our hopes for the future, and reacts critically upon false and inhuman schemes? This is a question of the ought. What technology *can* do is not necessarily what it *ought* to do—unless man be robotized and become a slave to the machine. At this point Christians and the resources of the Christian Church must be committed to the processes of dialogue and decision which bear upon the future of mankind. Their pictures of true humanity and true community are seen through the prismatic of the person of Jesus *(Ecce homo)* and his apostolic community. The missionary task is to make these images driving and alluring forces in universal history. Karl Rahner has stated, "It is, sadly perhaps, possible to show that the Christians of this day and age occupy themselves far too little with the programming of man's future in this world, as if this did not present any problems or could safely be left to the non-Christians."[20] It is also Rahner who has given to us a new definition of Christianity as the religion of the absolute future.[21] Roger Garaudy, the Marxist philosopher, has stated that this is a language Marxists can appreciate, "for the future is the only transcendence which those of us atheists who confess ourselves to be Marxists can acknowledge."[22]

We cannot here explore all the evidences of the anticipatory thrust toward the future which modern science finds running throughout nature and history. Karl Menninger is often referred to as an "apostle of hope" in the field of psychoanalysis because he stresses that hope is at the heart of a human being and an indispensable ingredient of personal therapy.[23] The voice of hope says there is a way out; hopelessness says, "no exit." As there is a psychology of hope,[24] there is also a biology of hope. This has been known for a long time. Thomas Aquinas ascribed the germ of hope even to animals, since they are moved by natural instinct to direct their actions toward the future.[25] But it is Father Teilhard de Chardin who carried out this idea most impressively in modern times. He saw hope as the essential impulse in keeping life moving onward and upward.[26] The only belief in God that Teilhard could accept was one which included faith in the future of the world. Teilhard thought of movement in the universe—cosmogenesis, biogenesis, anthropogenesis—in terms of the attracting power of the future. The Omega Point is the *Dieu en-avant*, the God ahead of us, the future goal of the world and mankind. Here we have symbols which can be helpful to Christian theology today, although at times Teilhard's *Dieu en-avant* bears too close a resemblance to the Prime Mover Unmoved of classical metaphysics. There is reason to question whether this God possesses the freedom of Yahweh in relation to the world and human history. Teilhard's idea of the future suffered from an ambiguity he never cleared up. In speaking of the future he oscillated between a teleological conception which he took from philosophy and an eschatological view which roots in the Bible. Teleology may be seen as secularized eschatology. In Teilhard's thought Christian eschatology is biologized, and biology is eschatologized, and this accounts to a large degree for the mysterious attraction of his thought to many Christians with a scientific orientation.

Christian eschatology and secular futurology need to be correlated but not equated. They are not to be equated particularly when the future is thought to be the extrapolation of the past or the extension of the present, as in much technological futurism. A crucial difference between secular futurology and Christian eschatology is this: the future in secular futurology is *reached* by a process of the world's *becoming*. The future in Christian eschatology *arrives* by the *coming* of God's kingdom. The one is a *becoming*, the other a *coming*. This difference can be illustrated etymologically by the German word *Zukunft*. *Zukunft* is a translation of two different Latin words, *futurum* and *adventus*.[27] *Futurum* is what grows out of something that already exists, hidden away in it as an inner potentiality. An oak tree is the acorn's *futurum*. All that is needed for the future to be reached is more growth, development, maturation, actualization. If this model is applied by theology, then the kingdom of God is something that is reached at last by speeding up the process of the world's becoming from within. The kingdom of God comes when the world comes of age. This yields the secularized idea of the kingdom of God in the nineteenth-century doctrine of progress, against which the theology of crisis in the twenties roared its protest (Barth and Brunner). *Adventus* is the arrival of someone or something new, which cannot be extrapolated out of history as such. This something new can be anticipated, hoped for, prayed for. The *adventus* of the kingdom of God is not a hidden quality of the past as such, nor is it a dimension of depth in the present. Speaking of the advent of the future in the language of hope is possible because the promise of eschatological revelation has become historical event in the person of Jesus. To speak rightly of Christ is to speak eschatologically of the advent of God's future, of the coming of his kingdom, in the open field of world history. Because of the future of God in the history of Christ, it is possible to hope for the future of the world in the kingdom of God's fullness. In this way the future in secular futurology and the future in Christian eschatology may be joined. The *adventus* becomes, for Christians, the basis of a *futurum* for the world.[28] Christians who anticipate the future of God's coming kingdom, on the basis of its proleptic occurrence in the Christ-happening, may work in the world with joy to toll the bell of hope.

The broadening of the horizon of modern theology to let the theme of the future be its guiding star will call for a realignment of tradition. Tradition is hermeneutically essential, for the events of the past are handed down to us through tradition. If any of them happen to be glowing anticipations of the future that is still out in front of us, we had better come to know that as soon as possible. But there are many traditions in the history of Christianity. A new focus on eschatology will stir up old and faded memories about eschatological radicals whose writings were suppressed by the official orthodoxies of their time.[29] Some back payment on accounts long overdue may be in order. In part this is a historical task. The kingdom-of-God tradition in Christianity needs to be made more accessible. Early Christian chiliasm, Montanism, Joachimism, the left-wing Reformation, apocalypticism in Pietism, sectarian millennialism, Christian utopianism, religious socialism, and present-day Pentecostalism, to mention a few of the major isms, are too often presented as simple miscarriages of the Christian message. In our more immediate American background there is the need to reestablish vital contact with the kingdom-of-God tradition in America. H. Richard Niebuhr wrote the history of this tradition,[30] showing how it resulted in the social gospel movement. This movement was all too hastily scuttled by neoorthodoxy because it preached, in Niebuhr's classic statement, "a God without wrath [who] brought men without sin into a kingdom without judgment through the ministrations of a Christ without a cross."[31] It would be a mistake to let these clever phrases blind us to the positive insights of the social gospel theology. An eschatological refocusing of theology will invite us to renew its attack on "the God of stationariness,"[32] its passion for the future of society, its anticipation of the kingdom of God as the revolutionary force in Christianity,[33] and its call to Christians to be advance agents of God's mission in the world.[34]

The new orientation to the future will also open up a new perspective on the achievement of Paul Tillich in America. There is no doubt in my mind that Tillich is America's most important theological import of this century. But one may doubt whether America was ready to receive Tillich's best. The last part of his *Systematic Theology* dealt with "History and the Kingdom of God." He wrote and published it at a time when he had lost the feel for the revolutionary dynamics of this theme. It was a job that had to be done to complete the system. His writings in the twenties and very early thirties were aflame with passion for the triumphs of God's kingdom in history. Tillich's social and political writings, his analysis and assimilation of Marxism, his interpretation of history and nature, in short, his whole religious socialist period, were driven and shaped by his eschatological views. When Tillich came to America he lost the social and political grounding of his eschatology. So he turned his attention more to the individual and his *Angst* in the postwar situation. Vaguely it was known that Tillich had been a religious socialist, but that was all in the background now. At any rate, he earned his accolades in America as a theological depth-analyst and existentialist free-lancer, interpreting cultural phenomena in terms of their transparency to personal and existential meanings. I do not belittle this American phase of Tillich's career. However, if we keep in mind the social and political dimensions of Tillich's earlier kingdom-of-God theology, I doubt that we would wish to dismiss him as "the indispensable comforter of those who grew up in a faith they can no longer believe."[35]

Today we face radical choices. To many it seems the horizons of the biblical message and modern culture are moving further apart through the process of secularization. The main hermeneutical bridges connecting the horizons are collapsing. Confessional traditions are experiencing that the pillars supporting their liturgical and dogmatic bridges are cracking beneath the weight imposed on them. Perhaps a new bridge can be built by sinking its shafts deeply on the one side into the bedrock of eschatologized history, namely, the future of God in the Christ-happening, and on the other side into the heart of man's hope for the future, namely, into the futuristic thrust of modern culture. Thus, doing theology as eschatology within the context of secular futurology delineates the terms of a possible new coalition that might help Christians of our time to become the spearhead of God's revolutionary movement in and for the world.

ONE

The Phenomenon
of Hope - Man

1. A CRITICAL PHENOMENOLOGY

In his *Critique of Pure Reason* Immanuel Kant stated: "The whole interest of reason, speculative as well as practical, is centered in the three following questions: 1) What can I know? 2) What ought I to do? 3) What may I hope?[1] By placing hope third, Kant may have intended no reflection on its rank of importance. But hope has languished in third place or lower on the agendas of modern philosophy and theology. This lack is being rectified by Ernest Bloch's philosophy of hope. His is a philosophy with a conscience for tomorrow, a bias for the future. With him philosophy is a learned hope *(docta spes)* which presses us to acknowledge the ontological priority of the future mode of being.

Hope is at the heart of existence. It seeks an outlet at every level of human life. Where there is life, there is hope. And "where there is hope, there is religion,"[2] says Bloch. We will add: where religion becomes total hope, there is Christianity. A total hope is one that is founded on the arrival of the absolute and

finalizing future of mankind in history. That is the message of
Christianity. As an eschatological message it is utterly and completely human. It does not lead us away from man, but toward the
perfect image of man in Jesus the Messiah. It does not direct our
attention away from the earth, because the greatest wisdom is
bound up with a cross staked in the ground and a grave dug into
the earth. It was Luther's most cherished conviction that we cannot drag God too deeply into the things of this earth.

Hope is not something tacked onto knowledge and morality
as a kind of superfluous emotional addendum. We do not begin
to hope only after discovering all there is to know and what we
ought to do. Hope is a primal thrust forward, underlying our
quest for knowledge and morality. Reason becomes abstract and
tedious, and the will to act immobilized and rigid, without the
catalytic agency of hope. This interpretation of man as a being
who lives by hope is based on a phenomenological analysis of
human existence.

In phenomenological analysis we look for meanings in the
original utterances and confessions of man, before they have become the building blocks of someone's (or the church's) speculative system. This is no slam against speculative or dogmatic
structures of thought. Rather, it is to recognize an elemental sequence, that myth precedes logos, that "the symbol gives rise to
thought."[3] We look for man's understanding of himself in the
world in his immediate and often primitive utterances, more than
in the eloquent speeches he makes at second or third hand. Man
is a poet before he becomes a propagandist; the mythmaker appears before the metaphysician.

However, there is nothing like a uniform image of man
which emerges out of phenomenological analysis. The symbols
and myths, legends and sagas, liturgies and songs, chronicles and
stories, in the history of religions do not yield a systematically
homogeneous view of man. Symbols and myths often seek to replace or destroy each other. The phenomenologist is not merely

interested in collecting and cataloging all these symbols and myths. He seeks to understand man in terms of them. But he cannot understand them except in terms of man. Hence, he is caught in what is today called the hermeneutical circle. He must have a point of view, an angle of perspective. No historian or phenomenologist looks at things from nowhere. A critical factor is involved in every analysis. This is required also by the sheer bulk of the material. It is this critical perspective at work in phenomenological analysis that makes it possible to cut through a mass of material and reduce it to intelligibility.

The critical factor which functions as a criterion of symbols is itself one of the symbols. It becomes the "privileged symbol" (Ricoeur) in one's analysis, not because of a blinding prejudice but by its self-demonstrating power to illumine and convince. Other symbols are arranged and interpreted in relation to it. If we understand man to be a creature who hopes in God as the power of his future, this is a picture of man which has been mediated through the history of Israel and has reached us through the tradition of the church. This is not a picture of man which descends on us from some outside authority, which we must accept on the authority of the Bible or the Christian tradition. This would make all phenomenological analysis into dogmatic propaganda. Instead, this picture of man must win its own way through phenomenological analysis. Therefore, our privileged symbol of man in history oriented toward the future is something which arises again and again out of the phenomena.

If we ask why a person chooses one symbol rather than another, we are brushing up against an ineliminably mysterious element in the decision of faith. At this point Christian theology has, sometimes too quickly, and yet quite properly, introduced its confession of the work of the Holy Spirit, who "calls, gathers, enlightens, and sanctifies the whole Christian church on earth," (Luther's *Small Catechism*). On the other hand, an appeal to the Holy Spirit does not work as a tool in phenomenological analysis, nor as an argument to prove the truth of our privileged symbol. To answer the question, why this symbol and not another, we are not reduced to muttering something about the decision of faith and the work of the Holy Spirit, as important as they are. Instead, we point to the phenomena, convinced of the inherent power and truth of one's privileged symbol. The symbol is not some dumb thing at which we have only to stare dumbfoundedly. It makes its appearance, it speaks to us, it comes with a judgment of its own. In phenomenological analysis we put our own privileged symbol to the test and invite others to see if our description is true to the way they too see things. It may or may not be, but if not, we always go back to the phenomena to look again, rather than rest deceitfully in smug self-assurance.

The critical factor in our phenomenological view is the primacy of hope in human existence. The classical slogan in Christian theology has been *fides quaerens intellectum,* or *credo ut intelligam.* Moltmann has suggested an alternative formulation, equally justifiable: *spes quaerens intellectum,* or *spero ut intelligam.* The motive in our quest for understanding is the hope which beats within us. This view of man as a subject who hopes, who lives toward the future, is one which is taken as a starting point, and then derived, expanded, and confirmed by phenomenological analysis. That describes the hermeneutical circle, which a person escapes only by standing nowhere. It is not a vicious circle, because we do not merely return to the point from which we began. There are degrees of *intellectum* that can be reached by the *spes* that moves within us. If the hope is right, if one's privileged symbol is not an arbitrary choice but has its reason in the structure of human reality, then this hope will pay high dividends in the sphere of understanding.

We have admitted that there is no pure phenomenology, without the intervention of a critical factor. We have also agreed that our principle of hope has been mediated through the historical experience of Israel and the Christian Church. However, as an eminently theological principle it is susceptible of a pretheological inquiry in a phenomenological anthropology. Philosophy and theology today meet at the level of a phenomenology of hope in human existence. This phenomenological step may become for theology today the "new style natural theology"[4] which John Macquarrie calls for, or the "transcendental anthropology"[5] which Karl Rahner proposes. This means that the methodological *prius* of an explicitly worked-out eschatology of hope is a phenomenological inquiry into the conditions in man himself which make it possible and meaningful to hope at all. If Christian theology should affirm, for example, that man must set his hope on God to be delivered from some predicament, some things are presupposed in making this statement and in expecting its meaning to be understood. What is being presupposed? How can the statement be accepted if it cannot be understood, and what would be the point of making it if we do not count on the possibility of its being accepted by those for whom this would first be received as new knowledge? Now this suggests that our slogan conceals the truth of a reverse movement, that understanding may be the pathway to hope, and better understanding to a brighter hope.

Before we plunge into the dogmatics of the church it is well to tarry awhile in the sphere of the profane (*pro-fanum*, outside the temple), where most people think their thoughts. A critical phenomenology may disclose that hope is not a theological virtue— to use the medieval scholastic term—which is solely a subject of biblical revelation and a quality infused in man by sacramental grace. That would, of course, make it an exclusive matter for exegesis and dogmatics. In the medieval period hope was forced to straddle the nature/grace dualism and was laden with the categories of substance and space. Thomas Aquinas acknowledged, of course, that hope is directed to the future, but the connection between hope in this life and hope for an afterlife could hardly be sustained in a two-story universe. In Protestant Orthodoxy the doctrine of hope, along with the future, could be found only among "the last things" of eschatology, whereas the other two theological virtues, faith and love, were emphasized on almost every page of its theology. This dwarfing of hope in Christian theology may be one reason that so many of the modern rivals to Christianity have been spawned in the Christian West. For if Christian hope and its future are relegated to an afterlife or a world beyond this world, there will be those who will create other symbols of hope to mobilize men for crusades in this life.

Where there is life, there is hope, and where there is hope, there is religion. I find these Blochian statements not only enchanting but of uncommon importance for a theology of the future. Hope is a structural element of human existence, of religion, and of the Christian faith. It is by exploring this linkage that it might once again make sense to think of Christianity as a true humanism, in spite of all past sins against humanity. The eschatological event in Jesus the Messiah, prepared for by the history of Israel and proclaimed by the apostolic community, is the core of a true humanism. But to make that meaningful as an answer to human beings, it is important to know what the question is. A critical phenomenology can help to illuminate the question, not to create the question or to derive the answer from the question but to formulate it in a picture of man as a being who lives in hope within the horizon of the future. Theology can then radicalize the question of hope, and thereby renew the conditions in man himself for hearing the gospel of the One "who gives life to the dead and calls into existence the things that do not exist" (Rom. 4:17). We have to face the truth: the gospel of the crucified and risen Messiah is nothing at all if it is not an answer to the question of man's hope for life.

2.   HOPE AND THE HUMAN CONDITION

The utterances of hope are signals that send out messages concerning the human condition. They tell us that man is like a ship suffering distress at sea while on its way to some destination. There are theories about man which claim there is no distress and no destination. We will disregard them for the time being, because our purpose is not to debate the naturalistic or absurdistic theories about man but to be instructed by the confessions of hope.

The message of hope is that man is in distress. Hope is an SOS signal. A person does not hope if there is nothing wrong or lacking, just as a ship does not dash off an ... --- ... signal except as a call for help. This says two things about the human condition: first, that man is aware of his being in distress, even to the point of fearing total shipwreck, and second, that man anticipates the possibility of rescue, searching the horizon from whence help might come.

There are many ways of expressing this bifocal vision of hope, the one bringing into view the human limitation, the other the possibility of overcoming it. The spectrum through which hope has expressed its awareness of the negativities in human existence corresponds to the varieties of religious experience (W. James). Poets and prophets, mystics and saints, have pioneered in exploring the depths of the human condition from which hope seeks deliverance. The French phenomenologist and philosopher Paul Ricoeur has taken the lead today in probing the negativities in human existence, in his studies dealing with major concepts like finitude, guilt, evil, fallibility, fault, etc.[6] A phenomenology of evil flanks a phenomenology of hope on its left side. It spells out the negative presuppositions without which hope would be meaningless. Hope lives in the tension from the negative toward the positive, from the sufferings of this present time toward a redemption that is longed for. There is always a correlation between the negative and the positive metaphors in every projection of the human situation. If we are in darkness, we hope for the break of day; if life is a tribulation, we long for relief; if we are stricken by illness, health is on our minds; if we are in slavery, we yearn for freedom; if we are exiled, our thoughts turn to the homeland.[7] In each of these situations, we put ourselves into our hope. And hope keeps our situation fluid, refusing to accept our plight as the last word, the final verdict. These metaphors are very general and seem quite bland. However, our purpose has been not to explicate a doctrine of sin and guilt but only to show how the phenomenon of hope glances back, as it were, upon the human situation, exposing and distilling in symbols and images the fissures within it. The more deeply charged metaphors of sin and guilt have arisen in their specifically Christian meaning within the covenant history of a people who face toward a living personal God, wholly free, righteous, and loving. This category of *coram deo* (before God)[8] intensifies the awareness of human deficiency, which all men to some degree share. It is the category by which one of the images of the human condition is elevated to the rank of a privileged symbol. But it is not unconnected with all the other symbolic projections of the human predicament in the history of religions.

A common accusation against the theology of hope is that it does not take sin and evil seriously,[9] because of its presumption to speak with hope and confidence for the future of mankind. Much recent theology has felt more akin to those who belittle hope and blaspheme the future, joining an elite of well-fed intellectuals, bedeviled by anxiety and despair. The accusation, however, is not on the mark, for hope is a wager quite well aware that the odds seem stacked against man. But hope refuses to accept the immediate hurdle as the end of the track, the present dungeon as a bottomless pit. Hope is an acute expression of the misery of man, but more, it is a protest against the weary spirit which capitulates before the "no trespassing" signs. These signs are placed all along the way by realists who are unquestionably in command of their facts. Hope is not a denial of the facts, but a refusal to accept them as the court of final judgment. Likewise, a theology of hope takes evil seriously, precisely by anticipating a power which can more than match it.

Hope counts on new possibilities which have not yet solidified into the hard core of established experience. No quarrel is necessary with an empiricism which decides to play the game by the rule of facts, only with a prevailing spirit of dogmatism which converts the facts into a universal formula which overrules hope, new possibilities, and the power of the future to free the present from the strangulation of the status quo. Hope reveals the kingdom of present facts as relative, open to change and to a coming future to which they might give way. This means that through the eye of hope the categories of freedom and future are grounded in the anticipatory structure of human existence. Hope is a meaningless act without presupposing freedom. To be free is to stand before possibilities, to transcend the present situation, to be able to change the status quo. Without this sense of freedom it would be senseless to hope, for hope would be crushed by an inner fatalism. Hope can inhabit only the one who believes the future is not a fateful repetition of the past or a mere prolongation of our pain and suffering. There is no limit in human existence, no foregone conclusion about the human situation, or about history, society, or nature, which hope can accept as an eternally sealed fate, predetermined by the way things have always been. The one who first said there is nothing new under the sun was not a wise man but a victim of an optical illusion. Hope simply does not regard freedom as unreal and the future as closed. To refuse to hope is an act of treason against man's essential nature which has yet to be established, which is still in the process of being created. If man is deprived of hope, he loses his freedom to go beyond the present. To lose one's freedom is to have one's future succumb to the crushing finality of the present and its bondage to the past. Hope is thus bound up with an awareness of time in which the future is a horizon of possibilities that are not mere projections of the past or predictions based on current trends. Hope is on the lookout for something really new, and will not model the future on the past and the present. It is hope that keeps alive the pioneering, venturing, creative spirit of man, which makes it impossible for man to wind the future so tightly into the present that the spring of life snaps or stops. Hope is the friend of freedom and the enemy of totalitarianism—in religion, morality, science, culture, and politics.

3.   THE CANCELLATION OF HOPE BY MYTH

Hope is not man's only possible response to the future. The unknowns of the future may quench hope, wither courage, and very likely evoke a response of anxiety and fear. When hope is driven out, despair takes over. Despair comes from *de sperare*— to be without hope. Anxiety in face of the future triggers off the attempt to find security for life in the past, to return to a paradise above time or at the beginning of history. It is anxiety that causes man to shed tears for the good old days, that makes him surrender his perceptions of the present and hopes for the future to his glorious memories of the past. Nowhere is this anxiety more conspicuously at work than in religion and politics. The utopias of hope are then slipped into the past and the mythical mood of "once upon a time" penetrates the religious rituals and political dreams. In Christianity this takes the fatal form of appealing to the faithful to remember some golden age, which actually did not exist in the first five centuries, as Anglicanism imagines, or in the High Middle Ages, as Roman Catholicism believes, or in the period of Luther and seventeenth-century orthodoxy, as Protestantism pretends, at least on anniversary occasions. Christianity is absolutely tied to memory, of course, but the genuine appeal to memory is a call of hope to remember the future which has been promised in the past and which the church is to prefigure through her faith and love in the present.

The deadliest enemies of hope are not, as one might think, doubt, despair, and death. Hope can cope with these; that is its mission. The deadliest enemy always appears with the friendliest face. In this case the friendly face is religion, not religion per se but religion as mysticism and archaism. The function of hope is

to keep faith active in history and to keep history moving forward
until the future itself overcomes the negativities of existence. Mysticism is an unhistorical way of thinking. What is truly real for
it is not what comes in and through history but what lies behind
or beyond the flux of time in the abysmal ground of being. Now
"ground" is a spatial symbol. Salvation comes by leaving the plane
of history, by sinking in this moment into the depths of the
motionless ground of being, into the eternal womb which sum-
mons all her children into formlessness.

In archaism we have the cancellation of a historical hope by
the myth of return to eternal origins. The biblical attitude of anticipating a new future far superior to any sunken island or lost
paradise in the past is incompatible with the myth of eternal recurrence. Yet, Christian theology is far from having drawn the
consequences of this incompatibility. In this myth we see the expression of a flight from history, and an inability to be sustained
by hope toward a future which has not yet divulged all its mystery.
Mircea Eliade has written the classical account of this myth of
eternal return.[10] This myth is the triumph of anxiety in the sphere
of religion. Only what is perennial is real; only what is repeatable
is meaningful. Religion is imitation and repetition of what possesses original, that is, archetypal, validity. Everything that counts
in religion must have been done from the beginning *ab origine*.
Religion needs to find its precedents among the ancestors; ultimately everything must go back to a sacred "once upon a time"—
in illo tempore. Salvation comes by suspending the duration of
history, just as in mysticism, and by participation in a timeless
event in a mythical epoch. Eliade observes that the whole intent
of this myth is to abolish history, to cancel time, to live in an
eternal present, by making the future nothing more than a recurrence of the past.

Corresponding to this mythical archaism is a futurism which
also abolishes the significance of hope in historical experience. Not
every attention to the future can be reconciled with the Christian

eschatology of history. A futurism which tries to overcome anxiety by taking a leap out of the present should not be confused with the futurism of Christian hope which presses for change all along the line. Some Christian theologians, Origen, for example, adopted the Platonic axiom that "the end is always like the beginning." This axiom is a rationalization of the mythical idea of eternal recurrence. Its symbol is the circle; it transposes into time the image of the cycle based on observing the seasonal rhythm of nature. If time is interpreted in analogy with nature, it is made to turn back to the beginning.

Another expression of this *Urzeit/Endzeit* axiom is the interesting fact that many of the great utopianists have located their ideal world in the past. Utopia is the creation of hope; it portrays "home, sweet home," and "happy days." All the negativities of existence are negated.[11] What then is the difference between utopian hope and eschatological hope? Both of them seem to use the principle of negating the negative and maximizing the positive in human experience. The contents are, therefore, often quite comparable. The difference is history. Utopias that are projected backward into some mythical past disregard the temporal dynamics of hope at work in biblical eschatology.

There has been a tendency in the Christian tradition, never completely victorious, of interpreting the entire history of salvation on the model of the myth of eternal return. Then the future is a correlate of the past, the end a restoration of the beginning, redemption a regaining of a lost paradise. The myth of the fall of Adam has misshaped the structure of Christian theology, not primarily because it was for so long taken as real history, but for two other reasons: first, because it was taken as an explanation of the origin of evil in the human race, and second, it was viewed as a "fall" from an originally perfect condition. Kierkegaard said all that needs to be said on the matter of explaining sin in the fantastic terms of a biological inheritance from the first ancestor of the human race.[12] Even more damaging, however, is the idea of Adam's fall from the perfect state of paradise. This places all later historical movement within the structures of the primeval past. Everything that is new is a recovery of the past; the history of grace is a restoration of a preestablished condition. Mankind is struggling in history to catch up to where it once stood in the figure of Adam. Eden is a paradise of archetypes; everything that happens later, so far as it is true, good, and beautiful, is an imitation and repetition of the original state of mankind. In the patristic tradition the Platonic essences were given an earthly embodiment in the way things were before the fall. The category of the old became virulent in Christian thinking, crowding out the place of preeminence that belongs to the new in an eschatological faith. The new began to be couched in words prefixed by a *re*. The history of Israel, of Christ, of the church, of the world, is going forward only to re-discover, re-collect, re-turn, re-store, re-vive, re-new, re-pristinate, and re-establish what existed once upon a time—*in illo tempore*. For the concept of hope, this means to cast it in the mold of memory. Memory in the Christian tradition was taken out of the biblical framework in which the initiatives of promise lead history into the open field of new reality. Instead it was placed in a Platonic cave where the shadows cause us to recollect an ideal world to which the events of history can contribute nothing really new.

In the tradition of Christian Platonism it was not at all essential to maintain the historicity of the myth of the fall. It was not modern historical science which first discovered the mythical character of the story of paradise, of Adam and Eve. Clement and Origen of Alexandria, for example, acknowledged without any hesitation that the early chapters of Genesis were not an account of historical facts. The myth could be dehistoricized, then ontologized in such a way as to retain the primacy of the original point of departure. It matters very little to real history whether it is made to proceed from a heavenly paradise above us or from an earthly paradise behind us. In either case, the essence of man is something ready-made, perfectly given in its original form and substance. Philosophically the primacy of origin is expressed in the slogan: Essence precedes existence. There is, I think, a sense in which the classical order must be maintained over the existentialist innovation: "Existence precedes essence." For the existentialist's point is not merely to reverse the Platonic order but to deny any transcendent point of reference in the self-determination of man. Existentialism is as inimical to an eschatological as to a protological orientation of man. On the other hand, from a historico-eschatological viewpoint, essentialism and its existentialist antithesis are both examples of antihistorical thinking. There is no room in either view for existence in hope toward a future determination of man's essence. History cannot really mean anything at all, if with existentialism the future of man's essence is collapsed into the present of his momentary existence, or if as in essentialism the future of existence is but a return to an already fixed essence. The choice between these twin philosophical options has been set forth in categories basically unrevised by the eschatological vision of reality as history whose truth is revealed from its future and whose meaning is not locked in the structures of what already is or always has been. The essence of a thing is neither in its past nor in its present but in its future. Man is an experiment in the laboratory of a history whose goal, according to the Christian hope, is new life in a new world.

4.   THE MEDIATION OF HOPE THROUGH HISTORY

Hope is able to outbalance anxiety as a primary posture toward the future only in the strength of a history which can provide a sufficient reason and right to hope. The God of Israel revealed himself as a God of history, a God of hope. The Scriptures are the record of the way that hope was won, of its struggle and victory over the hankering to go back or to stay put in present

securities. The life of Abraham, as Paul told it, was an exercise
of hope. Abraham is the father of many nations; he went on
hoping "when hope seemed hopeless."[13] He did not weaken,
though the impotence of his own body was exceeded only by the
barrenness of Sarah's womb. From this incident of hope in the
face of objectively hopeless conditions we have got our paradox-
ical expression "hope against hope." It means hope in spite of
hopelessness. Before that, Abraham had struck out on the path
of hope, walking with unarmed obedience and trust in the word
of promise. The call of the Lord began with an imperative: "Go
from your country," and was immediately followed by a promise:
"I will make of you a great nation."[14] A revolutionary turning
point! Life shall be lived by promise, breaking out of present
securities—country, kindred, and father's house—and going forward in pursuit of the objects of hope. This is the inauguration of
a biblical futurism that develops by stages toward the cosmic
eschatology of the New Testament. Here life is converted from
the closedness of monadic existence into the caravanlike openness
of a nomadic style of life.

With Moses, biblical religion took a further leap forward
into history. Moses' encounter with the Lord at the edge of the
wilderness was a religious experience with direct political consequences. The features of this story became landmarks on the way
to an eschatological hope with messianism at its core. A people
are in slavery, groaning under their burdens. A leader arises to
lead a rebellion. At this moment religion is used as a means no
longer to soothe the suffering but to transform it into action on
the way to freedom. Religion becomes exodus from slavery and
oppression. God reveals himself along the way by signs his people
cannot control, a cloud by day and a pillar of fire by night. The
God of exodus does not yet reveal him*self,* but rather he reveals
the way and the direction his people should go. He does not give
religion a center in a sacred place, but he gives a goal whose
reality can be known only by trust and hope in a promise. And

yet religion is not a state of emptiness along the way; there is manna enough for the day, and a lively hope for the land of promise flowing with milk and honey. The best is packed into the future. The two mightiest dangers in the present are: first, to grow weary of hope, by imagining full satisfaction in the present, relaxing the tension toward the futurity of the promise through the immediacy of false joy and dancing around a stationary god— a golden calf; second, to despair of the future, by yearning to return to the past, the land of slavery, the fleshpots of Egypt. The meaning of sin attains a temporalistic orientation: murmurings in the present, despairing of the promises that point to the future, and desiring to return to the past, even though it means the antihuman security of slavery.

The ultimate source of this dynamic futurizing of religion is God himself in the disclosure of his name in Exodus 3:14: *"Eh'je ascher eh'je."* This God of the exodus makes himself known as the God of the fathers, of Abraham, Isaac, and Jacob. But he does more than that; he gives himself a new name, which has usually been translated, "I am what I am." The medieval scholastics and today's neo-Thomists like Gilson and Maritain have seen in this name the biblical justification for defining God as "being itself," that is, for the ontologizing of the definition of God, already begun in the ancient church and carried through in medieval scholasticism. Modern biblical scholars, however, suggest that this expression *"Eh'je ascher eh'je"* is better translated as "I will be who I will be." The expression is ambiguous, and it is doubtful that anything can be clinched for theology by the underlying verb itself, *haja*. The Revised Standard Version is correct in allowing for both translations. However, from the context of a religion which moves from slavery to freedom, from exodus through wilderness to promised land, the futurist reading is to be preferred. As Ernst Bloch has stated, the futurist version sets off Yahweh's name from another name in the ancient world, that of Apollo. Above the door of Apollo's temple at Delphi the letters EI are engraved. According to Plutarch they stand for Apollo, the great "thou art, in the sense of a timeless, immutable existence of God."[15] Then Bloch correctly observes that Yahweh is entirely different; he appears as a God "with future as his essential nature. This end- and omega-God would have been foolishness in Delphi, as in every other religion, where God is not a God of the exodus."[16]

The whole Old Testament is a book of hope. This is so not only from a Christian perspective, which reads it as prophecy in light of the New Testament fulfillment. The religion of Israel, in its innermost essence, is hope toward the future in God. The Old Testament uses a number of words for hope: *batach,* meaning trust; *qavah,* to wait; *chasah,* to seek refuge, and *yachal,* to wait.[17] All of them have the meaning of hoping for something good, with the future in view.[18] There is confidence in this hope, mixed with eager anticipation, patient waiting, and seeking refuge. The book of Psalms is the prayer and hymn book of the people who place their hopeful trust in God. The ordinary reader of the Psalms today might well wonder what the Psalmist is actually doing by all his "waiting," an expression that occurs scores of times. He is not "waiting around," and he is not waiting in the empty sense in which Vladimir and Estragon are "waiting for Godot." The Psalmist is *hoping in God for our salvation.* He knows the One in whom he is putting his trust; he is not projecting his hope into a void, filling the picture of the future with wishes he knows are vain. His hopes are projections from the promises of God which have already been declared. He waits for God, that is, for a new congruity of reality with still unfulfilled promises.

The hope is fixed on God, true, but it is a pure abstraction when Bultmann declares that "hope does not always expect something definite, does not fashion for itself a particular picture of the future, but consists in a quite general trust in God's protection and help. Hence it can also be said that God is the hope, the confidence of the godly."[19] This interpretation of hope corresponds better with Bultmann's own existentialist concept of hope than it does with the Old Testament. In contrast to Bultmann's horror of objectifying language, the Old Testament has no difficulty in directing hope toward God and quite specific, statable promises. God is acknowledged and remembered in terms of his promises. As long as they have not been fulfilled, God's faithfulness and the believer's hope are on trail. When the Psalmist confesses, "For thou, O Lord, art my hope,"[20] he is not choosing between God and his promises, as though, like an existentialist, he had just experienced the horror of objectifying language. God is the believer's hope because only he can make good on his promises. And the future will tell whether God's coming is an act of faithfulness to the promises he has made. The Psalmist is straining forward in trustful hope, trusting in God at the same time that he hopes in his promises. It is true neither for the Old Testament nor for the New Testament that, as Bultmann maintains, what matters is not *what* we hope but only *that* we hope.[21]

In the prophetical books of the Old Testament the concept of hope is broadened and lengthened within the expanding horizon of an eschatological future and a universal consciousness of history. "In the prophets, despite all the newness of their message, the God who confronts Israel with his claims is no other than the *Deus spei,* the God of hope."[22] The hope which at first is for Israel[23] widens to one which includes all nations, until with the later apocalyptists, it embraces the entire world. The motive of the widening hope is the increasing intensity of God's proclaimed lordship over all nations and all things, and the severity of his judgment against all powers that challenge his supremacy and the ultimacy of his right. The serious hope of Israel is not founded on any notion that God is too squeamish to punish or man too good to be damned. Yet, its hope is striving toward a universal expression and precisely against the background of a belief in the wrath of God who says, "I the Lord your God am a jealous God."[24]

The hope of Israel undergoes lengthening in the encounter with death. The promise to which hope clings widens as the power of God is affirmed against all boundaries of life, and finally against the last boundary, death itself. But there is no clear ground of hope in the Old Testament in the face of death. It is as if a blank is left, to be filled in by later history, as if hope reaches only the threshold of an eschatology that grapples with the question of death. Toward the end of the Old Testament, in the apocalyptic writings, and increasingly so in later Judaism, the hope that encompasses death is focused on resurrection. How hope leaped forward onto a new foundation in the resurrection of Jesus will be discussed in a later chapter.[25]

5. RELIGION AS HOPE AND RELIGIONLESS CHRISTIANITY

Dietrich Bonhoeffer is being lionized today as the father of secular Christianity. Here we do not wish to take up a position either on Bonhoeffer as a whole or on the many rival interpretations of his thought. We will pursue only one thread within an essentially complex pattern of ideas. Bonhoeffer's assertions are by now well known, even to many who do not read books. He stated that the time of religion is over; soon there will be no religion at all. Men who are really modern cannot be religious anymore. Then, apparently alarmed by his own thoughts, and obviously expecting his friend Eberhard Bethge to be rather shocked by the new turn in his thinking, he wonders what this will mean for Christianity. How will Christianity make it in the future without being able to presuppose religion? It should be clear that Bonhoeffer's confidence never wavered concerning the future of authentic Christian faith. He was merely wondering about the new shape of faith in a time when men can do without, and are even better off without, any religion whatsoever. How can a person be a Christian without being religious? It has never been done before. How can the church preach its message and perform its mission without presupposing that man is by nature religious? This too has never been done before. "Then what is a religionless Christianity?"[26]

Bonhoeffer's phrase is a mare's nest of ideas. If the world, or the Christian, or the church, will exist "in an entire absence of religion,"[27] what specifically will they be doing without? Bonhoeffer did offer some help here, in using a wide assortment of specifiers, like inwardness, conscience, metaphysical presupposition, pious jargon, individualism, using God as a *deus ex machina,* as a stopgap, as a working hypothesis, inserting religion at the extremities of existence, at the points of man's weakness and immaturity, etc. The Christian in a "world come of age" will presumably still have faith in Christ, speak of God, but only differently, that is, in a secular fashion.

We have had a purpose in singling out the main terms which have become clichés in modern theology. Our purpose can be best formulated as a thesis. When all that Bonhoeffer meant by religion, as specified by these clichés, is rolled into an overall definition, it does not exhaust the meaning of religion. What we have in his definition is more like the perversion of religion, what the early Barth called "false religion."[28] There is an overspill of meaning in religion not containable in the definitions Bonhoeffer set forth to cover it. The phrase "religionless Christianity" is an intriguing combination of words whose reputation, however, is somewhat in excess of its merit when we consider the fact that all of the elements which Bonhoeffer poured into "religion" are easily unmasked as perversions from which Christianity would, indeed, do well to rid itself. To the extent that that is done, we are getting rid not of religion per se but only of the more perverted forms under which Christianity has masqueraded. And, when all the

perverted forms of religion are rooted out, then, it is well to re-
mind ourselves, the kingdom of God has really and fully come.
Then we will not need to pray, "Thy kingdom come." It will be
here. Then there will be not only no religion at all but no Christianity at all, and no need for faith or hope at all. The dream of
a religionless Christianity is an eschatological dream of the coming
of God's kingdom, and to that extent there is a sprig of truth in it.

Religion as hope will and must survive the radical surgery
that is needed today to be faithful to the gospel and alive to the
modern world. This is the overspill of meaning, in its barest
minimum, to which we referred above. We would wish to draw
our first argument from Bonhoeffer himself. Less than three
months after Bonhoeffer wrote his famous letter (April 30, 1944)
in which he began the amputation of religion, he wrote another
about the importance of hope in human life in general, and for
the Christian in particular. He had just read Dostoievsky's
memoirs from *The House of the Dead;* then he wrote to his
friend: "I am pondering a good deal on his contention (by no
means a passing phrase) that man cannot live without hope, and
men who are destitute of hope often become wild and wicked. It
doesn't matter if that hope be an illusion. It's true that the importance of illusion in human life is not to be underestimated,
but for the Christian it is essential to have a hope which is based
on solid foundations. However potent a force illusion may be, the
influence of a sure and certain hope is infinitely greater, and the
lives of those who possess it are invincible. 'Christ our hope'—
this Pauline formula is our life's inspiration."[29] About one month
before that, Bonhoeffer offered this insight: "The difference between the Christian hope of resurrection and a mythological hope
is that the Christian hope sends a man back to his life on earth
in a wholly new way which is even more sharply defined than it is
in the Old Testament."[30] If in these passages we have a sample of
religionless Christianity, taking the form of invincible hope, then
it is the kind of Christianity we also want. But why call it "re-

ligionless," as if religion, more than anything else, suffers from a perversion that lies beyond the scope of hope for redemption? There is a polemic of hope against false religion that goes back to the Old Testament prophets. These prophets did not float into a nebulous world of mythology or sink into unfathomable depths of inwardness. They had the spirit of hope active in history, and there is no reason of mind or heart to set that totally outside the compass of religion.

We have, however, more basic reasons to oppose the idea of religionlessness. Christianity is not discontinuous with religion, and religion, in turn, is not alien to the fundamental structure of human existence. The idea that the essence of Christianity has nothing to do with religion is one that was hatched by the very early Barth, in a moment of extreme aversion to the nineteenth century's tendency to subsume Christianity under a general definition of religion. In this case, any overspill of meaning in Christianity which could not be fitted into the "essence of religion" had to be removed. Bonhoeffer picked up Barth's criticism of religion, and only wanted to carry it through to completion. In fact, he criticized Barth for not finishing the job he was the first to begin.[31] Barth did not carry through his criticism of religion, for to have done so in an undialectical fashion, without affirming what is true and positive in religion, would have involved him in the same contradiction which, as we have shown, afflicted Bonhoeffer's own idea. For to write what Bonhoeffer did about the meaning of hope in human life and for the Christian, very shortly after having announced the end of religion and its removal from Christianity, can hardly be recognized as other than a contradiction. On the other hand, Barth's and also Bonhoeffer's fight against religion is not a contradiction as such when it is seen as carrying on the ancient prophetic attack on the Golden Calves and the Towers of Babel in the Bible and the Reformation. When religion is criticized in the name of Yahweh, its myths and magic, its demons and idols, are named and expelled. This criticism is not meant to be an operation so successful that it leaves the patient dead. The patient is man himself. As a victim of the perversion of religion, he needs a radical cure—the conversion of himself with his religion. Every book that has thus far been written on religionless Christianity has been a very religious book, the evidences of which as a rule fool no one but the author himself. In view of our definition of religion as hope, it is possible to call the bluff of those theologians who suggest that a universal indictment against religion per se would leave all that is essential in Christianity virtually unscathed or who propose a nonreligious interpretation of biblical concepts or who believe that the meaning of the gospel can be disengaged from speaking of God. The plausibility of any of these theological maneuvers rests on playing tricks with the word "religion."

We wish to make it unmistakably clear that a vision of religion as hope does not lead us into a general apology for religion. On the contrary, religion as hope is "religion against itself."[32] It is a painful polemic against forms of religion from which its most ardent devotees will never fully extricate themselves, until the coming of God's kingdom. There are forms of religion and of historic Christianity which rightly merit the eloquent funeral orations we hear today. If only we could dispense with these forms so easily! The perversions become more socially conspicuous by being concentrated in institutional structures, but they do not begin and end there. The perversions of religion are universally human phenomena, equally as tenacious and deeply rooted in the minds of people unconnected with specific cults and churches. A church is supposed to be a form of organized aggression against perverted religion, against the "manufacturing of idols," as Calvin expressed it. An idol is anything that blocks the way of hope, clouds its vision, and gives a false promise of security for the future. A church has no guarantee against idols; a nonchurch has none either. There are yet no signs that the "world come of age" is outgrowing a dependency on idols.

Religion is far from dead today. The so-called secular man is not without religion, although it is possible to abandon specific superstructures and epiphenomenal expressions often equated with religion. Our argument is not here primarily a sociological one, namely, that every society up to now has derived some coherence, order, and meaning from religion. Rather, it is anthropological; religion cannot die or even diminish unless man himself dies or diminishes. Religion can take many forms. When the forms begin to change, the initial response is to conclude that religion itself is on the wane. This is why religious professionals tend to be conservative. They are filled with anxiety, lest in tampering with the forms, the substance of religion itself leaks out. This anxiety must be overcome by hope, lest in refusing new forms, the norms of religion have a perverse effect on all life.

The religious drive is embedded in man as man. Man himself is the core of the religious concern. It is not the case that man merely asks religious questions, or that only some men ask religious questions which happen to be of no interest to others. This cannot be the case because man *is* the religious question. Religion as hope is a structural element of man himself. When traditional forms of religion are changing or dying, it is necessary to rediscover the radical humanness of religion in the phenomenon of hope. Not only is religion in man, but man is in his religion, as long as he presses hard the question of his hope, of his freedom, of his future, of his identity.

The liveliest religious question today is man's hope for the future. It is man himself, not some alien structure imposed from without, who is concerned for his future. In the Christian dialogue with the Marxist humanists of today, the vitality of this question of hope for the future has reached the front. The French Marxist Roger Garaudy states: "If you show that religion belongs *to man,* then we can talk to one another."[33] The answer to this is partly given in Ernst Bloch's assertion: "Where there is hope, there is religion."[34] What man expresses in his religion is his hope, his

longed-for future, his confession of <u>the difference between what</u>
<u>he is and what he ought to be</u>, his present existence and his not-
yet-present essence, the oppression out of which hope arises and
the salvation toward which hope aspires: happiness, home, fulfillment, life, peace, righteousness, freedom—in short, the kingdom of God. How much more religious can a man be than to
"hope against hope" for the realization of this kingdom whose
coming has been promised and certified by what the Scriptures
declare? The question is still the same old one with which Job
and many other pious Jews struggled: Are the promises valid?
There is no deliverance by hope alone, by hoping in hope, but
only in the promises of God, *if* they bring what they say.

The story of Jesus in the New Testament is grafted onto the
question of hope; it is told within the horizon of the eschatological hopes of Israel. After the crucifixion of Jesus one of his
disciples said: "We had hoped that he was the one to redeem
Israel."[35] On trial before King Agrippa, Paul testified: "I stand
here on trial for hope in the promise made by God to our fathers,
to which our twelve tribes hope to attain, as they earnestly worship night and day. And for this hope I am accused by Jews,
O king! Why is it thought incredible by any of you that God
raises the dead?"[36] <u>The validity of the promise and the future</u>
<u>of hope were for Paul bound up with the raising of Jesus from</u>
<u>the dead</u>. This is also what Bonhoeffer had in mind when he
wrote of "a hope which is based on solid foundations," and of
"a sure and certain hope."[37] It is only the truth of this hope
which can possibly distinguish it from illusion, which can prevent
Christianity from being just another perversion of religion.

TWO

The Power of
the Future - God

1. NATURAL THEOLOGY AND THE QUESTION OF GOD

Jesus of Nazareth is the person in whom the promises of the God of Israel and the hopes of men for fulfillment are joined. The question "Who is God?" arises out of man's concern for his future. It is simply a human question, as natural to man as the air he breathes and the bread he eats. There are as many answers to this question as there are religions. Christianity confesses God as Yahweh, the God of Israel, whom Jesus identified as his Father and whose coming kingdom he announced. The question "What is God?" is answered in terms of the promises of Yahweh to Israel. These promises were compressed and summed up in Jesus and his message of the kingdom of God. The identity of God is made known through the history of the promises of Yahweh to Israel, as they reach their point of concentration and fulfillment in Jesus of Nazareth. According to the preaching of the early church, the fulfillment of these promises in Jesus is for all men. They are universally true and meaningful for all nations, for all individuals, for all time to come. This means that the genuine hopes of mankind, through which the future of man's essence is expressed, are grounded in the promises of God. The hopes of men, and therefore their religious concerns, are gathered up and given a share in the realization of the eschatological promises of God in the Messiah of Israel.

The joining of the promises of God and the hopes of men in Jesus of Nazareth has become problematic in our time. It is not so much whether they should be joined in Jesus of Nazareth rather than elsewhere which seems to cause the difficulty, but whether there is anything to be joined at all. Who is this God? What are these hopes? Is not God an illusion? Are not hopes an escape? And if man has hope for the future, is it not a future which he himself must forge without God? The barometer of man's hopes seems to go up and down, from an opulent optimism to a pathetic pessimism, even among Christians, without any connection with their belief in God. It is our contention that where men seek a God without hope or their future without God, not only the foundation of Christianity but the very structure of human existence is being assailed. For religion as hope is the human quest for meaningful fulfillment beyond the present experiences of alienation and destruction within each individual and the whole gamut of life. Religion as hope is the question about the possibility of man's becoming truly fulfilled beyond the deformities of his past and present, and especially beyond the inevitability of his having to die. Man's hopes burst open his present, driving him beyond existing frontiers, searching the horizons for new reality. Man's hopes arouse his memories of reality that is no more, that has faded away into the stillness of the past. They give rise to the question whether the power of the future can reach also the past and connect it in wholeness with our present. If, as Ernst Bloch says, the key to human existence is to be found in the hopes which man holds for the future state of humanity and the world, then we ought to use this key to reopen the door to the message of Jesus. For Jesus' Father was the God of hope, who was about to keep his promises, to fulfill the hopes of mankind, by coming with his kingdom in the immediate future. If Christians today are to speak of God in any meaningful way, they must do it at the point where the promises of the God of history are revealed in Jesus as the answer to the truest and deepest hopes of mankind for fulfillment.

The question of the identity of God must become liberated today from all the counterfeit answers in the Christian tradition. When the word "God" falls on our ears like a big thud, it is primarily not because of a shift in world-views, not because man has come of age, with his science and technology maturing him beyond the need for God, not because of the empirical outlook of the secular man, not because of the horrific brutalities of the twentieth century, as much as all of these must be a challenge to any contemporary belief in God. There are two other reasons: first, the loss of the eschatological irradiation of meaning in the use of the word "God," and second, the collapse of the whole enterprise of natural theology. For centuries natural theology had been assigned the task of establishing the identity of God, prior to and apart from his self-revelation in Jesus of Nazareth. One could perhaps add a third reason. In compensation for the loss of natural theology, modern theology advanced with Karl Barth to a new christocentric definition of God. This was an important step; it gave back to theology its *norm* in christology. Yet it did so without reaching a new understanding of its eschatological *form*. It sidestepped the rediscovery of the eschatological shape of christology in Jesus' proclamation of the kingdom. The question of who and what and where God is was rightly answered by his self-revelation in Jesus Christ. Nevertheless, the word "God" was lacking its eschatological orientation and its definite connection with the question of man's hope for the future. Karl Barth rejected every form of natural theology, even in the restricted sense

[margin handwritten notes:]
Reasons for the emptiness of God's name in our time.

Note the role of importance which B assigns to natural theology.

of raising the question of God out of man's awareness of his own radical questionability.

The eschatological frame of God's self-definition in Jesus of Nazareth was replaced already in the ancient church by Hellenistic ontology. In this framework God revealed himself everywhere through the Logos in the world and in human existence. In Jesus of Nazareth he revealed himself more particularly as the Logos in the flesh. This basic pattern prevailed in the church's thinking in some form or other until modern times. The identity of God could be known apart from Jesus, apart from the history of Israel, by some form of natural theology. Classical Christian theology made a great investment in natural theology. This Hellenized form of natural theology, which can tell us who and what God is in advance of his own self-definition in the eschatological history of the Messiah Jesus, has collapsed. The "death of God" theology is, in one respect, only drawing out the more painful implications of this collapse.

What does the collapse of natural theology mean? It does not mean merely that the classical proofs of the existence of God have lost their argumentative force. It means rather that the classical media of general revelation, apart from God's self-definition in Jesus of Nazareth, are no longer felt to mediate knowledge of God. Ever since Kant, the media of a general revelation of God through the Logos in the world and in man have been getting less and less numinous and luminous. Even the question of the existence of God, let alone his divine attributes, is not clearly answered through the traditional channels of natural theology. Take nature, for instance. If once it communicated something stirringly suggestive to man about God, now it is quite exclusively the field for the experimental and controlling techniques of natural science. The heavens may still declare the glory of God, but the God whose glory they declare is not first identified by looking into a telescope. Theology at first resisted the prospect of losing access to God from the world of nature but then gave up in face of the overwhelming success of science. With nature gone, theology turned hopefully to history, as if there it could find, so to speak, the footprints of God in the sands of the past. History fell victim to the science of historiography under the aegis of a positivism which disencumbered itself of any God-hypothesis to explain historical causality and historical contingency. In its hands the facts of history become as dumb—Godward—as the phenomena of nature. The historian did not see God or the slightest trace of a God acting in history. God was no longer the real bearer of history; man was! Historical events, movements, and epochs can be understood, if at all, only as stories about man.

This description of what has happened to the natural theology is extremely valuable!

If theology loses history as a medium of the knowledge of God, along with the loss of nature, then the route of knowledge from the world to God is totally blocked. But there remains another way, from the inner experience of the self to God. God may be known immediately in the self, in the depths of subjective feeling. For some time this seemed to be an invulnerable arena. The word "God" was explicated by man's feeling of absolute dependence, to use Schleiermacher's term, or man's sense of the numinous, in the nonrational feelings of awe, dread, and fascination (Rudolf Otto). But soon the science of psychology placed its web of interpretation over these feelings and proceeded to explain every response without reference to the stimulus of God. When such feelings become overactive, the common opinion is that they should be taken to the psychoanalyst and that a healthy man ought to be cured of them.

By the same token, the moral dimension of human subjectivity need not be a medium of the knowledge of God. For a while it was hoped that the undeniable datum of conscience, the immediacy of the moral imperative, of the experience of oughtness or thou-shaltness, would be the divine *carte d'identité*. But we know what happened. As cultural anthropology analyzed the moral systems of mankind, it proceeded without the assumption of an unconditioned element underlying the relativities of experience.

A Kantian moral proof of God would be no more successful than the classical ontological and cosmological proofs, so far as these proofs are expected to establish the existence of God and therewith his identity prior to his self-revelation in Jesus of Nazareth. The death of natural theology signifies that its traditional channels of communication are no longer giving us knowledge of who and what God is—or even if he exists for sure.

The collapse of natural theology, however, does not mean that none of its classical functions can survive. A "new style natural theology"[1] is needed as a dimension within any Christian theology that bases itself on the self-revelation of God in Jesus of Nazareth. To be sure, it ought not create an image of God along-side of the history of God in Jesus the Messiah. That would after all be an idol worthy of destruction. Such a god would be but an extension of the world or of the self. Such a god is always a bor-ing succedaneum for the living God in whose name the first work of demythologization was done by the prophets of Yahweh. In spite of all that, however, natural theology is not irrelevant so far as it deals with the conditions in man and his world which give rise to the question of God. Nature, history, moral conscience, and numinous experience mediate an awareness of their own lack and their openness to a power which can promise unity, wholeness, and fulfillment beyond negativity. Natural theology today is a doc-trine not of God, of his being and nature, but of man in quest of his own identity and meaning, of the future of humanity and of the world. Man cannot cease asking the question of God. It is not natural for man to be an atheist! Christian theology must not stiffen to the point that its own premises place it at odds with the promises of God which have the needs and hopes of man in view. In asking the question of God, man will continually project images of reality, dream dreams, or make myths which purport to give an ultimate answer. Not these answers, but the conditions which give rise to the question, are of interest to a Christian natural theology.[2] Without an awareness of these conditions, the promises

Anthropol-ogy is the one great area in which natural theology can function meaning-fully today.

of God are spoken into a void. If man does not hope or need to hope for the coming of God, then what sense does it make for anyone to speak of God? Natural theology cannot tell us who and what God is, but it can trace out the contexts and conditions in human existence and in the world which correlate to the meaning of the word "God" when it is used. By way of natural theology we can establish the necessity, that is, the fundamental humanness, of the question of God, even though there is no longer any way of demonstrating the existence and nature of God apart from his self-revelation in Jesus of Nazareth.

If there are no needs in man and his world which still cry out to be filled, or if all needs can adequately be filled by man, then either God has become obsolete or the promised kingdom of total fulfillment has already arrived. Then not even the question of God will arise. The meaning of asking a question presupposes the need for an answer, that is, an awareness of a lack that needs to be filled. There are some theologians today who are trying to continue to talk about God while at the same time alleging that their God-talk is unrelated to any *needs* in man and his world. They have been frightened away from speaking of needs by Bonhoeffer's warning against the "God of the gaps." Any God who is invoked as the answer to human need is irrelevant in a world come of age. So they say. But is that really so? Presumably man no longer has any needs which he cannot handle. But while it is easy to say that, to the accompaniment of a loud chorus of voices chanting the slogans of the later Bonhoeffer, these same theologians have not made any headway at all in showing what sense it makes to speak of God. They may continue to speak of God for a while out of force of habit, but when the habit wears thin and they become inflated with the sense of having no longer any need for God, they will land, in effect, in the same camp with those who say "God is dead" or call the word literally non-sense.

In our view, the classical proofs of God may continue to stand as exemplary evidences of the power of the question of God.

The media through which a general knowledge of God was once derived may thus still mediate the question of God in the form of the questionableness of all reality and of human existence. Does this mean that apart from Jesus there is no knowledge of God? There are, of course, many *claims* to the knowledge of God apart from his self-definition in Jesus of Nazareth, as the God "who gives life to the dead and calls into existence the things that do not exist."[3] But there is no knowledge of God, and no acceptable claim to the knowledge of God, derived from natural theology or other religions, on the foundations of which Christian theology can build its own doctrine of God. The Christian doctrine of God stands or falls with God's self-identification in Jesus of Nazareth. This does not place the knowledge of God in strange isolation from all other reality. The *question* of God is not first mediated through an encounter with Christ. What is claimed, however, is that he is the sole medium through which God reveals himself as the finally valid *answer*. Jesus the Messiah is the exclusive medium of the divine self-revelation as the eschatological event of salvation. As the eschatological event he is the One in whom the final destiny of each individual and the ultimate future of all reality are represented. The meaning of inquiring after God and an understanding of what it means to speak of God can be reached by searching the human condition. But if Jesus of Nazareth is the *self*-revelation of God, then this is the eschatological event after which there need not be another such revelation of God. Jesus the Messiah is our hope because he is our future; he is our future as the eschatological event.

When Christians speak of God, they do not expect to be understood only by those who already believe. That would render preaching and verbal witness completely pointless. They expect others to be able to *understand* what they mean by the word "God," even though an *acceptance* of the truth of their assertions might come only later—coinciding with the act of faith. The task of natural theology is to enlarge the sphere of understanding so

[handwritten margin note: Natural theology, however, important as it is, cannot serve as the basis of a Xian theology.]

The question of hope provides the basis for a new approach to natural theology.

that when Christians proclaim God's identity in Jesus of Nazareth, the word "God" might carry some meaning between persons who do not yet share the same faith. By pointing out the phenomenon of hope in human existence, and by locating the essence of religion in the human question of the future of hope, we have achieved a possible starting point for a new type of natural theology. The great hopes of mankind may be embraced by the promises of the God of Israel, as they converge on Jesus' announcement of the impending future of God's kingdom. A person moved by the question of hope for the future may discover that biblical faith in God speaks that same language. This is the language of promise and future, of hope and fulfillment. As long as man has something to hope for, the message of the promise of fulfillment will get a hearing. Only when the kingdom has fully come, bringing the fullness of life, peace, and righteousness, will the agonizing question of God be silenced in the heart of man.

2.   JESUS AND THE POWER OF THE FUTURE

The Christian who can no longer identify God through the means of natural theology must come to the Father through Jesus of Nazareth. Jesus' God will be his God, or he will have no God. He will still be agitated by the question of God in the form of a quest for newness and wholeness, hoping for a future of identity in fulfillment. Thus, the God of natural theology is not dead; he is hiddenly active in the form of an unanswered question, anonymously present in the awareness of a new, fulfilling reality that does not yet exist. We can no longer proceed in the old way from a God we already know, whether that be the God "up there" or "back there" or "deep inside," whether the highest being, universal essence, or first cause. These gods of natural theology have lured believing Christians into a posture of atheism. These gods cannot promise or bring the fulfillment that man as man needs and hopes for. We do not already know who God is, and then puzzle ourselves over the question how so big a God can indwell or unite with so puny a thing as man. We do not have the same problem as the ancient christologists who wondered how the Infinite could become finite in the incarnation. For their Infinite Being was the God of Greek metaphysics who, of course, had to suffer a kind of ontological collapse to bring off a real incarnation.

If we bring our question of God to Jesus of Nazareth, we may let him show us his Father. "He that hath seen me hath seen the Father."[4] This is the favorite text of so-called radical theology, by which it claims biblical warrant to dispense with God, while keeping Jesus only. The text, of course, does not mean that we can have Jesus instead of his God. Rather it means that God has identified himself in Jesus. Jesus represents God to us. God the Father is united with Jesus as One who is different. There is not a unity of *dead* identity but a unity in difference. "Jesus" is not the name of a substitute for God. It is the essence of heathenism to make divine substitutes. The "God is dead" theology is a revival of heathenism on Christian soil, only blessing itself with the unction of a few Jesus-phrases. If we wish to refer our hopes to Jesus, we must see how he referred them to the approaching kingdom of God. Jesus did not draw attention to himself for his own sake. The claims he made about himself were entirely based on the authority of the kingdom of God. Jesus can define God for us, only because he first let himself be defined wholly by the future of God's coming kingdom. If we delete the reference to God and his kingdom in the appearance of Jesus of Nazareth, there is nothing left in Jesus to which we can refer our own hopes. And if Jesus can no longer define and mobilize our hopes, he is irrelevant to our future. Then "Jesus" is but an empty name, in no way exalted above all others.

Jesus defined God for us in terms of the imminent future of his kingdom. Jesus' God was Yahweh; he knew of the promises that had been given to Israel. He shared the horizon of hopes in Jewish apolcalypticism. All of these promises and hopes he packed into his preaching of the kingdom of God. The kingdom of God was the power of the future pressing in upon him, and through him upon his hearers. How can we today understand what Jesus meant by the kingdom of God? Do we have a contemporary translation of this term? Ours is an age in which kings have been dethroned. Kingdom-language is, therefore, bound to suffer from this general cultural shift away from monarchism. And who would wish to revive it? Modern exegesis has shown us, however, that the primary meaning in Jesus' idea of the kingdom of God was *power,* not realm. The age of monarchy was unable to understand the eschatological language of the New Testament. The most disastrous error was made when the church identified itself with the kingdom, as the territory ruled by a divinely established hierarchy. The empire-building notions in Christianity to date stem from this confusion, even when, as in Protestantism, its *de facto* hierarchy cannot claim to act by divine right.

The kingdom of God, as Jesus announced it, was awaited as the power of the future. Is this an adequate translation? We have already stated that the main motif in *basileia* was power. God's kingdom comes *en dunamei*—in power. But it was the power of God which Jesus anticipated from the future. In late Judaism and in the New Testament the word "God" was often replaced by "heaven." The kingdom of God and the kingdom of heaven meant the same thing. Power was something that came into our world from heaven above. But heaven for us today is a poor equivalent for God. As an attempt to symbolize the transcendence of God, it no longer irradiates much meaning. For us the heavens are not filled with the mystery and majesty of God, and we do not expect deliverance from above. The power which was then expected from heaven we await from the future. God's transcendence can be conceived today as the absolute power of the future. He comes to us not "from above" but "from ahead." And this accords better with the futurity of Jesus' own eschatological expectation.

When the Jews of the intertestamental period became reticent in using the name of God, they chose the symbol "heaven" as a translation of the divine name. We are in a similar position today of having to find a translation, not because the divine name is so charged with holy meaning but for the opposite reason. The tradition of natural theology affected a deeschatologization of the name of God. Its meaning faded with the loss of the futurity of its power. In addition to this, the Christian God gained a foul reputation by the established Christendom of our immediate imperial and colonial past. The name of God became part of "the cult of the absolute,"[5] invoked to guarantee the prevailing forces in society. The God whom Jesus proclaimed is not the guarantor of the status quo. He is the power of the future pressing for a radical conversion of the present.

Jesus did not offer a definition of God to which he later affixed an eschatological attribute. God is not a king in search of a kingdom. The being of God is his eschatological power. Futurity is essential to his very being. When Jesus said, "Seek ye first the kingdom of God," he fused the reality of God's kingdom into his being. God's kingdom is not something additional to himself, else we would have no business seeking it first. What God brings when he brings his kingdom is himself, in the power of judgment and salvation. The God who comes, who is anticipated, is the God of the Old Testament whose promises are fulfilled in the future of God himself. God is not other than his promises. That is to say, God is the reality of his Word, first in the form of promise, finally as fulfillment. The ancient church fought fiercely for the essential identity of God with his Word. Unfortunately, however, the dominant notion of the Word at that time was the apophantic Logos of Stoic and Platonic philosophy rather than the Word of promise in the history of Israel and the message of Jesus. If God is identical with his Word, this involves an eschatological unity between the content of the Word and the author,[6] so that the Word is not misunderstood as an eternal self-manifestation of a stationary God, but as the Word of promise through which a future fulfillment is anticipated. In this unity of the divine mode of being as promise in history and the divine mode of being as fulfillment from the future there lies the root of an eschatological conception of the Trinity. We will say more on this later.

God defined as "the power of the future."

As a symbol for God we prefer "the power of the future" over some others recently attempted, for example, Tillich's "ground of being" or "power of being." The reason is simply that "the power of the future'" is a phrase deliberately chosen to reactivate the eschatological orientation of Jesus' preaching of the kingdom of God, in which the being of God is identified with the power and the glory of his rule, now pressing in from the immediate future, whereas a term like the "ground of being" owes its life to the very mystical ontology (Neo-Platonism) which replaced the eschatological framework of early Christianity.

The power of the future became present in Jesus' ministry in a unique way. This sounds like an incautious assertion, in view of the unending debate in the New Testament field whether in Jesus' preaching the kingdom of God was expected in the future or was something already present. Sayings can be found in the earliest strata to support both sides. Some scholars attempt to reduce all the futurist passages to the present, to turn them in support of a realized eschatology, or simply to remove the more stubborn ones as editorial retouchment. We cannot here recap the debate we have summarized elsewhere.[7] In general, however, one cannot escape the conclusion that the facts are better known than loved. Hermeneutical interests more than exegetical findings are often at work to absorb the eschatological future into an existential present in Jesus' ministry. It seems hopeless and disingenuous to try to switch all the tenses onto one track or another. On the other hand, the counsel of *Heilsgeschichte* theologians, which has virtually crystallized into a new orthodoxy among moderate and conservative biblical scholars, that we must place the references to the present and the future of the kingdom of God side by side or one after the other, forming thereby a time line running from the present into the future, is not the only way of solving the problem of the juxtaposed sayings in a systematic conception. Agreed: it is not a question of either a present-tense or a future-tense eschatology. It will not do to overcome an eschatology that projects everything into the future, leaving a vacuum in the present of Jesus' own ministry, by a realized eschatology that assimilates everything to the present, making the future a dead end. The systematic question is this, as Moltmann has formulated it: "Does the present determine the future in extrapolations, or does the future determine the present in anticipations?"[8] It is, therefore, not enough to settle for a both/and formula, which retains the "already" of the present and the "not yet" of the future side by side in Jesus' message of the kingdom of God. A decision has to be made on how to understand the connection between the present and the future. There is a commonsense element in the standard *Heilsgeschichte* scheme, according to which, just as the power of the past has determined the present, so the power of the present will determine the future. But common sense can deceive. In the ministry of Jesus the power that determines all reality was awaited from the future of God's coming kingdom. The power of the future pressed for an unconditional obedience, radical receptivity to the new conditions of eschatological existence, and above all, freedom from bondage to the past. "No one who puts his hand to the plow and looks back is fit for the kingdom of God."[9]

The power of the future was present in Jesus of Nazareth without ceasing to be future. The kingdom was present through advance symptoms and premonitory signs of its futurity. Jesus did not go before his hearers with the information that there is such a thing as the kingdom of God; that would have been no news to them. What he announced was that the kingdom was drawing so near that its impact was already being impressed upon them through him. The eschatological day is dawning; its glimmerings are already breaking out in Jesus' works and words. It involves judgment. A person will be judged by his attitude to Jesus who is the fulcrum of the future, the place where the old is phasing out to make room for the new. Disciples of Jesus become partisans of the future, advocates of freedom and forerunners of newness. For to be free is to have a future. To believe in Jesus is to let him keep our future open for new things which the power of the future aims to release into our present. A man will be justified, therefore, through his relation to Jesus, if Jesus' claim to authority is not mistaken. The justification of sinners and the godless is linked to the eschatological judgment already proleptically enacted in Jesus' ministry. The Messiah Jesus is the believer's hope because through faith in him he, so to speak, pockets in advance a merciful verdict which he can anticipate *propter Christum*.

The effusion and efficacy of the power of the future in the person, acts, and sayings of Jesus constitute a real presence and union of God with him. This is a confession of the Godhood of Jesus that can only be made, as indeed it first came to be made, retrospectively in the light of Easter. None of the contemporaries of the historical Jesus called him God, not even his closest disciples. The power that was operative in Jesus was not even self-evidently God's. Some thought that Jesus was in league with Beelzebul, the prince of demons, and others demanded a sign from heaven, real proof of his authorization. Jesus refused to give a sign—"except the sign of the prophet Jonah. For as Jonah was three days and three nights in the belly of the whale, so will the Son of man be three days and three nights in the heart of the earth."[10] According to Matthew's account, then, the full eschatological certification of Jesus' pre-Easter ministry was bound up with the resurrection. The resurrection of Jesus acted like a magnet, drawing the exalted christological titles from numerous religious sources, giving the evangelists the means to discern retrospectively the swaying power of the eschatological future in Jesus' earthly ministry.

3. GOD'S SELF-DEFINITION IN JESUS' RESURRECTION

Christian hope is grounded in the resurrection of Jesus of Nazareth because through it God defined himself as the power of the future beyond the finality of death. Jesus' earthly claim to authority was not in itself adequate as the basis of Christian faith. The crucifixion of Jesus dashed the hopes which his announcement of the coming kingdom had aroused. A new event was needed to confirm Jesus' claim to stand for God. Though laying no claim to titles that placed himself directly on the line with God, Jesus had spoken and acted as though he were on the inside of God's will for the world. His encroachment on the authority of God, as the Jewish leaders felt so keenly, was a blasphemy unless his claim were legitimated, as Jesus himself expected, from the inrushing future of God's kingdom. Jesus was making claims and promises which he himself did not and could not fully keep in his lifetime. To be sure, he was already bringing eschatological foretokens of salvation in the concrete present. But in no sense was salvation realized by the poor and the meek, by the sick and the blind, by traitors and sinners, as though they had nothing further to await from the future of God's coming kingdom. Rather, Jesus' offer of salvation was a sample now, not an imitation but the real thing, of a future fulfillment of life in peace and joy, in freedom and righteousness.

The resurrection was an act by which God identified himself with the cause of Jesus, vindicating Jesus' claim to represent the future of God in his earthly ministry. At the same time, the resurrection was an act of God by which the cause of Jesus could be continued in history, as an ongoing promise in the life of mankind for a future share in the new reality which occurred already in the Messiah Jesus. The resurrection was thus the pivotal point by which God defined himself retroactively in the life of Jesus. This forms the root of the Christian doctrine of the incarnation, and ultimately of the later symbol of the preexistence of Christ. In the event of the resurrection God declared himself for Jesus, even as Jesus, a real and true man, had wagered his whole life on being the authorized anticipation of his Father's kingdom. Without calling himself the Messiah, he played the Messiah's role of breaking through the barrier between the old age and the new reality of God's rule. Likewise, God defined himself in the resurrection of Jesus prospectively by founding the mission of the apostolate and sending the eschatological community into the world with the message of a living hope. The resurrection is the door through which the cause of Jesus seeks and gains entry into the world.

Two things are of crucial importance in the resurrection of Jesus: that it happened and what it means. Nothing is more fatal to the Christian faith than to locate its meaning outside its happening. The resurrection is not meaningful, except as a comforting illusion can be meaningful, unless it really happened. Christian faith is a confession to the God of hope who "raised Christ Jesus from the dead,"[11] "who gives life to the dead and calls into existence the things that do not exist."[12] If God is stripped of this means of his self-identification, we can only count ourselves among those others "who have no hope."[13] Then we must fall silent about God, for to be without hope is to be future-less, to lose our trust in the power of God's future to meet us on the far side of our death. Christians have no other God than the one who creates new "life from the dead."[14] If they let go of the God who "raised from the dead Jesus our Lord,"[15] they will have only the God of wrath[16] and they will be left in their sins.[17] Then they can only join in Jesus' cry of Godforsakenness from the cross, and go to meet him in hell. This is a Black Friday Christianity without the light of Easter Sunday.

There has never yet been a Christianity which has not presupposed the resurrection of Jesus as the ground of its own existence. Likewise, there has never been any picture of Jesus which has not been portrayed backward from the event of the resurrection. The historical Jesus of the Gospels is painted for us in the colors of Easter. The early Christians remembered who Jesus was in terms of who he is; and who he is was acknowledged in terms of who he will be—as the one who yet comes. The risen Christ of Easter does not flood the stage of history with light, but he is the foreglow of the advancing glory of God that will shine through all things in the end. Hence our knowledge of God's final self-definition, the future of Jesus' own cause, and our mission of hope in the world are all grounded in the resurrection of Jesus.

In affirming the event of the resurrection, we are not offering a theory to explain it. What is basic to the Christian hope is that it happened and what it means, not how it happened. The urge to explain it, however, will never subside. Explanation is a dimension of understanding we always seek. Nevertheless, it would be foolish to hold that an explanation is needed to gain access to the life it promises. That would be like refusing to watch television until one could explain electricity, or refusing to admit one had fallen in love before explaining how it happened. If it is a theory one wants, there is plenty of choice, from the subjective (R. Otto) and objective (H. Grass) vision hypotheses to the physicalistic (fundamentalism) and spiritualistic (modernism) theories. One of the latest is Tillich's restitution theory.[18] I prefer a transformation theory according to which the total being and meaning of Jesus of Nazareth—whatever it is that made him not only human but the particular human being he was—was transformed to a new mode of reality, appearance, and expression, so that as the living Lord ahead of us, our forerunner, he leads forward the work of transformation that now goes on in history, at the forefront of which the church is called to participate. Yet, whatever our theory, we must return again to the New Testament records, and not invent facts to fit our theories, or devise theories that conflict with the historical witnesses we have in the New Testament.

The whole New Testament speaks of the event for which the

symbol of resurrection stands when it says that Jesus who was killed on a cross is no longer dead but is now alive. The event by which Jesus moved from the state of death to new life was called resurrection. There were, however, no witnesses of this event. What we can say for sure as a historical fact, in the currently narrowest sense of this term, is that there were witnesses who claimed to have seen Jesus after his death. The one who had been crucified appeared to them as the living Jesus. The stories of Jesus' appearances and the witnesses' seeing do not all harmonize. Nevertheless, their common underlying datum is this occurrence of having seen none other than Jesus under new conditions of his presence and action. Those who had this experience reached the immediate conclusion that if the crucified Jesus is really living, God must have raised him from the dead. How could they have done so? They were in no more of a habit than we of calling someone dead alive. Yet this became something of which they could not be more convinced, so much so that they were ready to lay down their lives for it. Of course, their martyrdom does not prove its truth, but it moves people to take their assertion more seriously than otherwise they might have been inclined to do.

Peter and the Twelve, the many other nameless ones, and last but not least of all the witnesses, Paul, were able to speak of this surprising occurrence of seeing Jesus alive after his death as God's act of raising him from the dead because they already shared the resurrection hope in late-Jewish apocalypticism. They already had the language of resurrection before the event. They did not invent a symbol for a new variety of religious experience. The event did not initiate the language; rather the language of hope was already prepared beforehand as the symbolic means to interpret what was happening before their eyes. On the other hand, the event did not happen just as they had been led to expect. They revised their preresurrection hopes in light of Jesus' appearance. A first revision was necessary because they had anticipated the resurrection of all mankind at once, and not that of one individual by himself. The second revision was needed because the resurrection of the dead signaled the end of history, but history was running on indefinitely. The conclusion was this: the kingdom whose future coming Jesus had proclaimed and anticipated in his earthly ministry took a strange turn by occurring in Jesus' resurrection before the end of history. But in happening at all, it was an eschatological event for all men—a promissory note of future fulfillment to all those who invest their hope in God's Messiah.

The logic of hope is based on the resurrection of Jesus as an eschatological occurrence. There is nothing in it for hope if it is no more than a freakish return to life of someone who has died. For then, like others who have been revived after dying, Jesus would still have to face death in his own future. Jesus is the pioneer of hope because he overcame the deadliness of death once for all, by being raised into union with God, who creates something from nothing and life from death, as the absolute power of the future. When the disciples and others saw the crucified Jesus, they were faced with an either/or. Either this was a miracle of revivification within the prevailing conditions of this age, in which case Jesus, like a Lazarus, would still be enclosed by death, or this was really the event of resurrection, just the break they were looking for, beyond the enclosure of death.

Unless we too grasp Jesus' resurrection as the eschatological occurrence, as the beginning of something really new, we end by dealing with it as a miracle in analogy with other miracles. Then we either affirm or deny it, without realizing how little it means either way. The resurrection of Jesus is not an answer to the question whether a dead man can return to life, but an answer to the question whether the crucified Jesus is now living in union with God, not only for himself, but as our representative who has gone ahead to prepare the way for us.

The resurrection as the eschatological occurrence is the point of transition to our speaking of Jesus as our Judge, our Savior, our Lord. Take the event of the resurrection away from the structure of Christian faith: then Jesus is not our index to God's final self-definition; then we look forward to a new revelation for which Jesus was only one of the signs along the way; then we are still standing in the Old Testament situation; then the basis of any christology at all is undermined. For the resurrection event is God's confirmation of the christology implied in Jesus' own claim to authority—"But I say unto you!" If we remove the confirmation, the claim loses its validity. This means that the resurrection is an interpretation with a manifold meaning. To be sure, it does express the conviction of the early church that the cause of Jesus continues even now and has a future (W. Marxsen); it does express the significance of the cross as a salvation-event, depriving death of its power (R. Bultmann); but before it does that, it interprets the appearance of the crucified Jesus as the eschatological act of God.

The resurrection is not a symbol of interpretation that can be freely exchanged for some other, in expressing the contemporary meaning of Jesus. That would too easily dissolve the event-character of the resurrection, reducing it to a symbolic way of speaking of the immortal influence of Jesus' life, the power of his faith, or the courage of his dying. The resurrection is not an interpretation without an event of its own to interpret. It does not only refer back to Jesus' life or his cross. It refers to an event "on the third day." The meaning of this phrase secures for the resurrection a content of its own that cannot be transferred to something else— say, back to a quality in the historical life of Jesus or forward to the subjectivity of faith. It stands as the link connecting both. Faith and Jesus fall apart, just as God and Jesus fall apart, without it. But since God has raised Jesus from the dead, as we believe, he has given us a good reason to hope for life in spite of the "axe of annihilation" (Bloch) that is poised above us all.

4. RESURRECTION HOPE AND THE DEADLINESS OF DEATH

Resurrection hope is "the conviction of things not seen,"[19] pointing us ahead to "what we do not see."[20] We do not see how we can find fulfillment in a world in which "the jaws of death crush all things."[21] Death is the final hurdle over which hope stumbles. We know we have to die and yet we wish to hope. But "death, conceived as the axe of annihilation, is the most stringent of nonutopias."[22] What should we do? We must hope, not just for this or that but for the final future of our own identity, in communion with all those whom love embraces. Yet how can we hope in face of death? What is there to hope for from death? If death is our eschaton, how can we not slip into radical hopelessness? How can we evade nihilism? How can we neutralize the poison which death releases into life, driving us to exploit each moment as our last, at whatever or whosoever expense? The quest of life in face of death is for a power that can swallow it up in victory.[23] Those who say that the reality of death poses no problem to them are fooling themselves. That is, of course, one way of handling the problem. We can fool ourselves as we often do. We can drown out the voice of death by a clatter of noises; we can run from it; we can beautify it by giving it a look big as life itself; we can invent euphemisms like "passing on" and "going home." There is no end to the things we can do. The ploy of the secularist, who of late has found some theologians to bear his torch, is that death is merely a biological incident, an episodic phenomenon, the fear of which we lose as soon as we objectify it under the glaring light of scientific analysis. Of all the silly things that are said, surely the silliest is that "modern man is no longer afraid of death." As a statistical matter, some are, some aren't. As an existential matter, the modern man has scarcely gained any advantage over his most primitive ancestors.

The most familiar solution to the problem of death is to place the soul of man out of its reach. This is what Ernst Bloch calls the "extraterritoriality" of the core of existence (the soul) in relation to death and nothingness. Religions specialize in painting pictures against death. The idea of the immortality of the soul, of its transmigration, or whatever, has been since Plato the classic expression of this attempt to satisfy death with only the outer shell of the soul. But death wants and gets more than the outer shell. It penetrates to the inner core of existence, cracks it open, and takes all there is to take. The solution of Christian hope to the problem of death is not to try to negotiate a settlement, hoping that the enemy will be decent enough to acknowledge the infinite value of some immortal part that is "extraterritorial," beyond its jurisdiction. The only extraterritoriality that Christian hope knows is the life of the resurrected Christ who brings victory through and beyond death. We cannot pluck any hope from death; we cannot deny death's reach and reality; we cannot count on a deathless element inside of us. Instead, we affirm the deadliness and finality of death as the inescapable outcome of our lives. But that is not all we do. We anticipate a new beginning. We look at death as that which has already once met its match. We see the darkness of our own death illuminated by the light of Easter. "By his great mercy we have been born anew to a living hope through the resurrection of Jesus Christ from the dead."[24]

The hope of resurrection concerns the individual. In an age of collectivism the tendency is to translate individual hope into the social process. But the promise of a better society in the future is not a real fulfillment of the individual, as long as an individual is not reducible to his social function. A person is more than his social role. Resurrection hope, as the Bible proclaims it, is pressing on toward a totally human and fully personal fulfillment. On the other hand, hope is not limited to a fulfillment of individual persons. The individual's solidarity with his community and men's solidarity with the world of nature make it understandable that resurrection hope will rebel against every doctrinal restriction which sets fixed limits to its vision. Can a hope that is nourished by the promise of Christ's resurrection and filled with agapeic love ever err on the side of hoping too much?

Jesus' resurrection makes our history the time for hope. This hope is anchored in God's future, which has been revealed in raising Jesus from the dead. Since this future is not only the future of our present but the future of our past, our hope looks forward to a fulfillment of our past, because our present will also join our past as that which is no more. Christians remember the past hopefully as that which is reconciled to the present from the power of their common future. The power of God to raise the dead includes the power to gather up the broken, unfulfilled past into a new creation, so that at the end "God may be everything to every one."[25]

THREE

The Presence of
the Future - Jesus

1.   THEODICY AND THE CROSS OF JESUS

The cross of Jesus was the great theme in Luther's theology. *"Crux sola est nostra Theologia."*[1] Luther was echoing Paul, who wanted to know nothing "except Jesus Christ and him crucified."[2] But what can a theology of the cross mean this side of the resurrection? Did not Easter cancel Good Friday? Has not Christ already been enthroned as the heavenly Kyrios? Does not Christ now reign as the risen Lord and give us already a share of his victory? Should we not rather have a theology of glory, if eschatology has already been so magnificently realized? What does it mean, then, to have a theology of the cross if Jesus has really been raised from the dead?

One ploy that is sheer deception is to boost a theology of the cross as a *substitute* for a theology of the resurrection, while pretending fidelity to Paul and Luther. Needless to say, the polemic of the cross in Paul and Luther was aimed not at the resurrection but at a theology of glory. The essence of a theology of glory is to think and act on a fully realized eschatology—to have and not to hope. Then all that we could hope for has already been realized. "For who hopes for what he sees?"[3] Such a thought leads to ecstasies of fulfillment in theology, knowing too much (gnosticism) in the church, claiming too much (triumphalism) in religion, pretending too much (perfectionism) for the times in which we live. A theology of the resurrection must be allied with a theology of the cross. The risen Jesus is present in our not-yet-fulfilled world in cruci-form. The resurrection was not for Jesus an exit from our brutal world into heavenly bliss above. It is not the story of how one man made it through enemy lines and now waits peacefully on the other side to see if others will get through. The first witnesses identified the risen Jesus by the marks of his crucifixion. The body of the risen Jesus can be identified by us in the bruised and bleeding body of mankind with which he identified himself.

The theology of the cross presupposes the resurrection of Jesus. It was only in the light of Easter that the cross arose as a *theological* question. If God has raised Jesus from the dead, this is an eschatological event which confirms Jesus' own claim to be an advance agent of the coming rule of God. But why did Jesus have to suffer and die? Why did God abandon the One whom we now confess as his only Son, our Lord? Was the cross only an unfortunate incident, a bad mix-up at city hall, perhaps just the obscene fate that may greet anyone who sticks to his ideals? There was no obvious answer for the early Christians. The cross of Jesus was not self-explanatory. It was not expected that resurrection must be preceded by a cross. And when the disciples saw Jesus being crucified, they did not relax and say, "It's just a question of a few days, and everything will turn out all right." The sequence was this: If Jesus has been raised, why was he crucified? What is the meaning of the cross? It was not this: Since Jesus has been crucified, he must soon be raised. The first Christians did not talk as easily about the unity of cross and resurrection as has been done in recent theology.[4] Cross and resurrection did not fit together like hand in glove. The cross was more of a problem than the resurrection, precisely because it could be posed as a theological problem at all only on the basis of the resurrection. Except for the resurrection, the crucifixion was like one more hanging in our day, perhaps unjust and to be deplored, but not too much riding on it. The event of the cross was not accompanied by a prior symbol of anticipation by which the meaning of the event could immediately be brought out of it, as in the case of the resurrection.[5] This is all the more evident in view of the form-critical finding that Jesus' passion predictions are *vaticinia ex eventu*.[6] Jesus did not go to his death following rubrics that he was reading off some script. Jesus gave the first believers his life, not a ready-made theology of the cross. To answer the question "Why did the risen Jesus have to suffer and die?" they searched the Old Testament for clues to bring out the meaning of Jesus' death on the cross. And they found *inter alia* the Isaianic image of the suffering servant.

Here we touch one root of the problem of theodicy in the Christian faith. If Jesus was what he claimed to be, and if God has confirmed that claim in the resurrection, why did Jesus have to suffer and die? Why did God lay this upon him? God must be justified—*theos-dikē!* But there is another root, arising out of the eschatological origin of the Christian faith. If Jesus' resurrection is the eschatological event of history, why does the crucifixion of life still go on? If the end has come, why doesn't it look like it? If Jesus is what God claimed he was by raising him from the dead, then why do we have to suffer and die? Where is the fulfillment of the promise of life, the kingdom of peace, freedom, and righteousness? Why did it come so hiddenly, if it came at all, that no one can see, feel, or enjoy it? Why, if the Messiah has come, has not the world been changed? Why have there been two thousand years of church history, marked by complicity with the killing of Jews, the gassing of innocent children, the tyrannizing of the weak by the strong? Why is mankind still being nailed to a cross? Something is radically wrong. God must be justified, or man or the world, or all three. If Jesus is the eschatological event of salvation, the Messiah of God, he must be the place where God justified himself, or where man and his world are justified before God.[7]

Theodicy is not the seemingly abstract question of the Enlightenment thinkers who debated why an Almighty God created a world in which there is physical, moral, and metaphysical evil. And the answer is not that this is the best of all possible worlds (Leibniz) or that a little bit of evil is needed to magnify the good. The question of theodicy is why the dawning of eschatological fulfillment in Jesus' life, death, and resurrection was arrested. Why did not Jesus' resurrection trigger off the succession of events which had been promised in the day of eschatological fulfillment? Of course, this problem does not arise except on the eschatological premise of Christian faith. If the eschatological hope is not of the essence of Christian faith, then we may suppose that we can shake loose an ethical kernel from the eschatological husks. That course has been tried without success. The essence of Christianity lies in its eschatological core, not in some ethical ideal, as our whole argument has shown up to now. And this is why the question of theodicy is a burning issue. Why does the agony of existence continue, if the key event of future fulfillment has already occurred once in Jesus' resurrection from the dead? This is the much-debated problem of the postponement of the parousia. What is the meaning of life during the time of postponement? This is not identical with the universally human question about the meaning of life as such, in view of all the evil in the world. That was Albert Camus' question, and of many existentialists today. The Christian's question is posed by the contradiction between his eschatological faith and his existential experience. Because the fulfilling future of mankind has drawn so near that we can already anticipate its shape in the new reality of Jesus Christ, why does God not deliver us from evil? Why must we take up a cross to follow him? Why does he not remove the cup of bitter suffering from the sons he claims to love? We would have thought that Easter would bring us someting better than we have experienced. Human beings kill human beings; the gentle are ravaged by violence; the beautiful are raped by lusts of ugliness; Jews are victims of racial sadism; mature Christians voted for Nazis; men of science and technology built the gas chambers of Dachau, created instant death for thousands in Hiroshima and Nagasaki, and produced napalm to melt the bodies of women and children in Vietnam. Black people are despised and rejected by whites, and hate them for it. We would have thought that Easter could do us better than that, that with it we could have expected a new heaven and a new earth, an end to tears and pain, to mourning and death.[8] It is the sheer incongruity between our faith in the God who defined himself at Easter and our experience of unfulfilled reality that raises the question of theodicy in the peculiarly Christian sense.

This experience of contradiction between our resurrection faith and our human situation drives the Christian to the cross of Jesus. It is important to see that the motive for a theology of the cross arises precisely from this contradiction. It did so for the early Christians. Their theology of the cross grew out of the postponement of the parousia, after the initial ecstasy of Easter faith was challenged by the hard facts of human suffering and death. The old situation was still overlapping the new. Easter did not cancel Good Friday after all. The risen Lord is still present in our time as the crucified Jesus. We gain an ever deeper knowledge of the resurrection of Jesus when we immerse ourselves in the mystery of his suffering and death. The resurrection did not lead Jesus into eschatological glory beyond the pale of human suffering and dying. Easter enthusiasm was brought down to earth by the preaching of the cross. The danger was, as with the Corinthians, to float off into another world outside of time, to abandon the earth on which the cross of Jesus was staked. They did this through cultic immersion in the presence of the eternal. They had a realized eschatology of glory.[9] A theology of the cross after Easter means that God's presence and human suffering are brought together. The answer to the question of theodicy must be sought in the representative meaning of Jesus' death on the cross.

2.   JESUS: GOD'S REPRESENTATIVE AND OURS

The cross of Jesus was the crown of a life lived totally for others. Jesus' death on the cross has representative significance. He died *for us*. That is the simplest expression of Christian faith, underlying all theories of the atonement. But the death of Jesus was not an isolated act of representation. Jesus' entire life had been representative of the coming kingdom of God, bringing its healing power to the sick and the dying, its forgiveness to sinners and outcasts, and new hope to the poor and powerless. The cross is not a special mechanism of salvation apart from the whole self-surrendering service of Jesus as God's anointed delegate in a world of antidivine powers—sin, death, and all kinds of evil. The cross was the destiny of a life which dared to anticipate the reality of God's love, to stand in for God by granting unconditional forgiveness and freedom for life already in the present. Jesus' act of representing God before God established his kingdom in power resulted in God's self-identification in the weakness of the cross. God accepted the cross of Jesus as a sign of his own creative, suffering love. The cross of Jesus represents the depths of God's love to us. The crucified Jesus is the presence of the future of God under the conditions of alienated existence. The coming kingdom of God's love pours itself into the cross, adopting it as the form of his presence in the midst of a suffering, dying, and godless world.

In Jesus' cross God identifies himself with the pain of mankind and its experience of Godforsakenness. The cry of Good Friday is still the cry of mankind: "My God, my God, why hast thou forsaken me?" The whole earth stands in the shadow of the cross. Jesus takes our experience of Godforsakenness, the atheism and nihilism in all of us, into his own cry unto God. And in spite of that experience of being forsaken by God, he hangs on: "My God, my God."[10] Jesus would not forsake God. That is why Jesus not only expresses our Godforsaken feelings, but can also be the One unto whom we cry in our Godforsakenness.

Jesus' cross is the incarnation of God's future in a loveless world and therefore the inauguration of a future for man in the fullness of God. An exchange occurs in the cross—from God to man and from man to God. A theory of the atonement which boasts of an exclusive theocentricity short-circuits the truth that Jesus is also man's representative before God.[11] God has delegated him to be both his representative and ours, by raising him from the dead, by identifying himself with Christ's suffering, and his pain with ours. Faith is an act of letting Jesus be our representative, of letting Jesus' death be *for us,* so that we may hope to share in his victory, find reconciliation with God through him, and live even now the life of freedom that the power of love can bring. In the resurrection Jesus has gone ahead of us, pioneering our future. In the cross Jesus stays with us, participating in the suffering of our present. The risen Lord is the crucified presence of the future which God is still struggling to carry through to victory.

As our representative Jesus does not replace us.[12] On his cross he died for us, but not instead of us. We still have to suffer; we still have to die. His suffering and his death are not a substitute for ours. When we speak of the vicarious cross of Jesus, this means that his death is a service to our benefit. We no longer have to die as if he had not preceded us. We no longer have to die alone on a Godforsaken hill "outside the gate."[13] We can die in a communion of his love, in the assurance of the forgiveness of sins, with undying hope for life and resurrection. Because he died the death of the sinner as the sinless, he can be our representative. Because he died the death of the guilty as the guileless man, he can be our representative. Because he died the death under the law as the man of love, he can be our representative. He can be our representative because in his resurrection God accredited him as the One who has what we lack, and who lacks what we have. He has the right credentials to be the ambassador of the human race before God. He is the new man of the future. His resurrection to lordship gives us his counsel and leadership. He goes before us to God, pleading the case of mankind, to make room for it in the future. He made his case with his life and his death, remaining absolutely faithful in the service of God's coming kingdom. The question Jesus' cross put to God was whether God would accept his life of creative love as the sufficient basis to continue his own hope in the human adventure.

The life and death of Jesus have been so exclusively controlled by incarnational thinking that it is difficult for us to view his real humanity as something more than a christological category. Jesus is viewed from the start as God walking around on earth or as the Son of God descending into the guise of human life. This thinking from above to below claims a "high christology." But it is one-sided. It undercuts the element of contingency in the historic existence of the man Jesus of Nazareth. It makes history simply the unraveling of a ball of thread that has been manufactured elsewhere. History is the theater of God's decision, not the platform where he announces some eternal decrees. Jesus had to earn his right to be the representative of mankind. His were real temptations. Only to those who enjoy a superlook from a timeless tower of eternity was he not able to sin (*non posse peccare*) because, after all, he was the incarnation of the Son of God. The Gospel writers did not know that much, and so they presented his life as a risk and struggle on the way to becoming through his suffering and death the representative Man for all men. It was not all part of a plot decreed in advance, so that Jesus had only to follow a flawless script. His unity with God was perfect, but not automatic.

Along this line, we accept an element of adoptionism in christology. The incarnational approach has never fully succeeded in expunging it from the Christian tradition. To be sure, adoptionism has always flirted on the borders of heresy, but not without being able to appeal to some support in the New Testament itself.[14] The abiding meaning of adoptionism is its witness to the thoroughly and historical character of the life of Jesus. Only if Jesus was really human can he go before the Father representing us as his brothers.

But now we must turn our thinking around, and stress that the cross of Jesus was an act by which God represented his participation in man's suffering. As God's representative Jesus does not replace him. He is not a substitute for God, filling in for him while he is away on leave. His suffering is not in place of God's suffering. It is rather the place where God himself shares most deeply in the suffering of all mankind. To believe in the cross of Jesus is to let God suffer with us. We do not believe in an impassible God—a God who is stone cold in his heart of hearts toward the suffering of his creatures. Only a suffering God can help.[15] It is rather unfortunate that the ancient church got itself into a doctrinal bind in the Sabellian controversy, so that it had to condemn Patripassianism *tout court*. Ever since then, orthodox Christians have been afraid of speaking of the suffering of God, although not to do so creates a bizarre image of a Father who identifies himself with Jesus as his own son, without letting himself in on any of his pain and suffering. To believe in a God who does not suffer great pain in a world of pain must mean that ours is a Greek deity for whom motion itself is most painful. But the Father of Jesus, the God of history and hope, is not in himself motionless self-identity, unmoved by the pain of those with whom he relates.

Man needs one like Jesus to give his cause a chance for fulfillment in God's own future. As Dorothee Soelle puts it metaphorically, "We need Christ so that God should not 'sack' us.

Without Christ, God would dismiss us on the spot."[16] Likewise, God needs one like Jesus to make his own case credible in a world of pain and death. For what good does it do that he raised Jesus from the dead if he does not translate that victory back— as faith, hope, and love—into the life we live here and now? Again Miss Soelle gives us an apt metaphorical expression for it: "For without Christ, we should have to 'sack' the God who does not show up, who has left us."[17]

When we do not hang on to the connection between God's presence and human suffering in the cross of Jesus, we are without faith. When we do not believe in the connection between man's future and the resurrection of Jesus, we are without hope. Cross and resurrection bracket the life of mankind. The cross which bears the stench of death is the good news of God for our living. The resurrection which carries the signature of life is the good news of God in our dying. Whether we are living or dying, we have faith and hope, because God has identified himself with with Jesus, and Jesus with us. And Jesus has identified himself with God, and we with him.

Jesus is the representative in whom God and man exchange hope for each other. Because of Jesus' cross God has a reason to hope for man; on account of Jesus' resurrection man has a reason to hope in God. For Jesus' sake we do not give up on God, and he does not give up on us. That means that Jesus has opened up the future for both God and man. He is ahead of us by being accepted into unity with the Father; he is ahead of God by advancing into our present in the form of suffering love. We do not have to live any longer in a world sheltered by idols and illusions to satisfy our unquenchable need to hope, nor do we have to live in this secular age as if God were dead ("*etsi deus non daretur*"[18]). We can do without idols and we can do without the dead gods of the past. But in Jesus we meet the living God, the Lord of the future, the always coming God, the God ahead of us, who proves himself to be God by raising up life from death. As long as those who live shall die, and as long as those who die are dead, God's God-hood will always be a matter open to question. Job's question will rise up to haunt us. Jesus holds the future open for hope in a God who will still prove that he is God by raising all the dead, filling the whole transfigured earth with his glory. It is the task of hope in the risen Lord to cut through the darkness of Good Friday and the shadows of death to a confident faith in the power of God's future to make all things new and to bring them to fulfillment in the "homeland of identity" (Bloch).

3. THE KINGDOM OF GOD AND HIS RIGHTEOUSNESS

The raising of Jesus, we have said, was God's confirmation of Jesus' earthly claim to represent him and his coming kingdom. It was also the revelation of Jesus' death on the cross as God's participation in the evil and suffering of the human race. Thus, the life, death, and resurrection of Jesus are together rightly called the event of salvation, and Jesus is therefore addressed as our "God and Savior." For only God can save, and not man alone. The saving reality that Jesus brings into the present is the rule of God's righteousness. Righteousness is the content of God's coming kingdom. All the great salvation-words in the Bible— reconciliation, redemption, justification, forgiveness, regenera-tion—are grounded in the power of God's righteousness that has found expression in the new reality of Jesus the Messiah. This righteousness is all-encompassing—justice for the community, justification for the individual, and judgment for the world. These combinations of terms can, of course, be rotated—justice for the individual, judgment for the community, and justification for the world. The righteousness of God is the power of crisis and new-ness in all human situations.

The New Testament has often been read as a book with at least two messages: Jesus' message of the kingdom of God and

Paul's message of the righteousness of God. Many a split in church and theology can be traced to this Jesus-or-Paul dichotomy. H. R. Niebuhr's famous judgment against social gospel Christianity offers an ironic reminder: "A God without wrath brought men without sin into a kingdom without judgment through the ministrations of a Christ without a cross."[19] But if a theology of the kingdom has often been escalated into utopian enthusiasm, a theology of the cross has equally often resulted in quietistic resignation in face of the powers of evil that hold sway in this world. And a radical Paulinism of wrath, sin, judgment, and cross has often detached itself from Jesus' preaching of the kingdom of God. Cross and kingdom go together. The Pauline Christ who is the righteousness of God and the Synoptic Jesus who announces the coming kingdom are one and the same. For righteousness is the content of the kingdom. The gospel of the New Testament is the message of both the *basileia tou theou* and the *dikaiosunē theou*. We should declare an end to the competition and seek a correlation between the kingdom and cross motifs in the Christian tradition.

The righteousness of God is not a divine attribute which merely becomes revealed in Christ. "The widespread view of God's righteousness as a divine attribute can now be rejected as misleading. It derives from Greek theology which speculates about the attributes of God."[20] The righteousness of God, his justifying grace or reconciling love, in that case would be an eternal attitude of God's mind toward the world. But history is not the place where God merely makes known his timeless and unalterable attitudes; it is the means by which God reaches new decisions, makes up his mind, and alters the trend of things. God's righteousness is revealed as that which is realized in the obedience of Jesus in his surrender of himself on the cross, and in his resurrection to new life beyond death. He "was put to death for our trespasses and raised for our justification."[21] God's righteousness is the crisis of the old and the creation of the new. It is a happening in history which creates a new situation, not only subjectively on man's side but objectively in God's relation to his world.

When God's power takes hold in his Messiah Jesus, it brings resurrection to him and righteousness to us. The divine power in his resurrection releases new energies to set things right on earth. Righteousness is not an idea which God entertains in his mind. It is a power to stir things up, to shatter imprisoning conventions, and to break new trails of freedom. Jesus anticipated the reign of righteousness in the future of God. "Seek ye first the kingdom of God, and his righteousness."[22] Käsemann has established that Paul's idea of the righteousness of God has its background in the Old Testament and in Judaism, within the same horizon of expectations as Jesus' preaching of the kingdom.[23] The power of the future in Christ is the dominion of God's righteousness and lordship. The future of God's rule meets our world in the righteousness which God establishes throughout the world in the cross and resurrection of Jesus. This is a divine righteousness which in Jesus seeks the rights of man, puts things right between men, and makes things right between men and God. The righteousness of God is for Paul "a noun of action, which does not describe God as he is in himself but God as he reveals himself."[24] God's righteousness is his power in relation to men who are not in the right, who do not do what is right, who violate the rights of others in self-righteous aggression, who rob God of his rights, his due, by putting him down in their pride.

The power of God's future becomes present where righteousness reigns on earth. The core of this righteousness is justice infused with love. Where love is not able to do its work freely, it uses the instruments of law, threats, and punishment. Luther spoke of this work of love through law as God's strange work—*opus alienum*. God puts on the ugly mask of his wrath to pressure people to satisfy the needs of others, even when they do not feel like it. Men do not freely live for others; they live for themselves. There is a deep perversion in man. His aversion to God takes the form of preventing the future of others by seeking to use them for his own present security. There is a sluggishness of the will, so that even when a person wants to do what is right for others, he does not always do it. The power of God uses the pressure of law to get men and their institutions heading in the right direction. Of course, there are also powers at work to prolong the present and prevent the future, to keep things as they are. Laws become unjust when they freeze the present in the interests of some at the expense of others. God is a pressure for justice in human society, seeking new laws which cause men to serve each other. The core of justice is care for the neighbor.

The kingdom of God cuts into history as a two-edged sword. We cannot get beyond speaking of God in terms of Luther's "law of contrasts,"[25] even when we cannot simply repeat Luther's words. God works under contrary signs—of strength and weakness, wisdom and foolishness, law and gospel. There are contrasting ways of God's working in the world. God is hiddenly at work in the world behind our backs. As Luther said, the great rulers of history can be made to do the will of God, even against their will; they are God's dummies.

The phenomenon of law in history is an instrument of divine justice, confronting man in his actual empirical existence. God is active through the law within the structures of social and political life, whether man recognizes it or not. Man's consciousness of God is no index of his power and presence. Kings and dictators and democratic assemblies are instruments for carrying out the political purposes of God, whether they know it or not. There is no sphere of life where God is not active through the law, seeking always more ample forms of justice and love. No man can be an "outlaw" in a complete sense. For the law works not only as an external form but as an internal pressure, however ambiguously. God is universally present as a pressure driving men to do right, to give to others their due. Life could not go on for a moment without the pressures which God exerts behind the back of every individual. This law of God as pressure for greater justice is a driving force behind the demands which human beings make upon each other as they live in community. These demands do not come written on tablets of stone from the heights of Mt. Sinai. They come from behind and below, arising from within the always new situations which the historic community of mankind faces. Laws are not statements of an eternal will but instruments on the way to the goal of the universal righteousness of God's kingdom. A situation ethic is correct, but only on the ground of its eschatological function in history. A law is judged to be good in a given situation if it opens the future for a greater fulfillment of persons in a true community of love.

The image of God as the universally present pressure—the anonymous demand[26]—in, with, and under all situations of life is not a bit of natural theology that stands apart from the image of God as the power of the future. For the universal pressure is no longer anonymous for those who confess his self-definition in the Christ-event. The anonymous demand is not the law of another God, just as the Father of Jesus is not other than Yahweh, the author of the law which Jesus fulfilled in righteous love. The meaning of the law is revealed by its goal. Along the way it is subject to massive distortion and abuse as an end in itself. Our view of God as the hidden pressure for justice in the world is oriented to the enactment of his righteousness in the eschatological event of Christ. If the law is used as a way of salvation, it leads to self-righteousness and constricts the rights of men. Hence Jesus' conflict with the custodians of the law. The purpose of the law is to make way for a fuller and freer future of man.

The righteousness which God finds wanting in men he brings in Christ as a gift of pure love. There is no way into the kingdom of God except through righteousness. And since there is none righteous on his own, each must enter the kingdom with the righteousness of another. The future of God rejects everything as its adversary that refuses to seek the fullness of life for others.

Jesus is the representative of God and man in his living and dying for others. God accepts those who enter his future with the representative righteousness of Christ. On account of Christ we are declared righteous!

With these assertions we enter the heartland of the Reformation. Usually they are summarized as the doctrine of justification by grace alone, received through faith alone, on account of Christ. This is a doctrine that many today feel is irrelevant to the concerns of modern man. If justification answered to Luther's deepest existential question, it does not mean much today. There is obviously much truth to this. The Helsinki assembly of the Lutheran World Federation (1963) tried to reach a contemporary formulation of the basic concern of the Reformation, but the theologians fell all over their words disputing fine points—a sure sign that the doctrine has passed from its existential youth to its scholastic old age. The "Message of the Assembly" stated: "The man of today no longer asks, 'How can I find a gracious God?' His question is more radical, more elementary: he asks about God as such, 'Where is God?' He suffers not from God's wrath, but from the impression of his absence; not from sin, but from the meaninglessness of existence; he asks not about a gracious God, but whether God really exists."[27] If the Lutherans cannot make much sense out of the Reformation message of justification for the modern man, who else can?

There can be little question that the juridical language about justification does not resonate in modern ears. But how about righteousness? How about talk of the rights of man? Demanding one's rights? Being in the right? Seeking and doing what's right? If the righteousness of God in Christ is the promise of the world's future, might not those who crusade for the rights of man here and now turn with a listening ear? Is it really true that modern man is not interested in righteousness?[28] Perhaps not directly the righteousness of *God,* but is the aim of God's righteousness really something else than to establish the rightness of man in the end?

When God declares his righteousness, it takes shape as a man among men, the true and new manhood of the coming future. God's righteousness is a power which brings future salvation to men in the present, setting things right even now as a sign and signature of final righteousness to come. This righteousness is not a substance or attribute; it is a new relationship beginning already now, freeing man to use his powers in the care of others. If I know that my future is assured, taken care of, I need waste no energy worrying about it.

The Reformation message of justification has suffered terribly in its transmission through Orthodoxy and Pietism. It is perhaps not so much modern men who cannot grasp Paul's message of the righteousness of God as it is modern sons of the Reformation who rebel against intuitively felt distortions in the traditional doctrine of justification. Believing in the true doctrine of justification by faith alone became a good work of the mind, a righteousness which orthodox believers could boast of—and did—before God and man. It also became part of a psychological scheme of salvation—the *ordo salutis*—which could be traced as the work of the Holy Spirit in the subjectivity of the individual. Justification was one station along the way of becoming subjectively a good Christian.[29] The process toward subjectivization in the *ordo salutis* was begun in the period of Orthodoxy and completed in later Pietism. This whole development has collapsed. Paul's powerful message of the righteousness of God was "grace for the world,"[30] not an event in the interior development of the individual. Paul's message must be freed from its captivity to "the introspective conscience of the West."[31]

A reformulation of the personal, individual meaning of justification can be had only when it is rooted once again in Paul's message of the righteousness of God. The category of the individual with his existential experience does not provide the primary focus. Christology (cross and resurrection) and not anthropology (conscience and conversion) is the first matter of interest to Paul.

The total message of God's righteousness for the world cannot be translated into the framework of an existentialist individualizing anthropology. Existentialist soteriology is a modern form of the earlier pietistic reduction. The righteousness of God "for Paul is God's dominion over the world, which is being revealed eschatologically in Christ."[32]

It is equally important to resituate the doctrine of justification in its eschatological horizon. From Melanchthon to Karl Holl and beyond we have had the most rarefied discussions about whether God's justification consists of a purely synthetic and forensic judgment of "declaring righteous" or also an analytic judgment of "making righteous." Karl Holl sneered at the forensic idea as a "legal fiction" contrary to God's fine sense of morality. It is quite common to hear such sneers against the idea of justification as a forensic act of God by which he imputes to sinners the alien righteousness of Christ, and so regards them as wholly righteous, in spite of the fact they still have no righteousness of their own. But why the sneers? Is it the cold juristical language that offends? Or do we have here the *hubris* of the sinner uttering blasphemy? Or is this either/or (either *declare* or *make* righteous, either *impute* or *infuse* righteousness) a debater's delight, an issue on which he can marshal as many good arguments for as against? If we look at the issue from an eschatological angle, which was Paul's own, then the forensic categories of merit and law do not take over.

The righteousness of God in Christ becomes proleptically present as salvation for the world without ceasing to be future. That is, it can never become an object we possess in our present. This is the truth of the forensic theory of imputation. Righteousness is not something we can now have subjectively as a possession. This does not make it a "legal fiction" but always keeps it also an object of hope. No one stressed more than Paul the real presence of God's eschatological future, yet it was he who confessed, "We wait for the hope of righteousness."[33] He also said, "Not that I have already obtained this or am already perfect. . . .

I do not consider that I have made it my own; but one thing I do, forgetting what lies behind and straining forward to what lies ahead."[34]

The controversy about "declaring" and "making" righteous can be settled in terms of Paul's distinctive "proleptic eschatology."[35] This is a concept that has not only been worked out in systematic theology by Pannenberg and Moltmann but has also received solid exegetical support from Käsemann and Stuhlmacher.[36] We have as we hope; hope is the form of our having the righteousness of God, whose final realization for the world is still a matter of the future. "We have it," Käsemann says, "under the sign of promise and expectation. . . . Even the gift of divine righteousness places us not at the goal but on the way. It is given us in such a way that it at the same time always lies ahead of us and must be grasped anew."[37] The grace of God's righteous love is near and present precisely as God's eschatological future is near and present—proleptically present, in the form of promise. "But according to his promise we wait for new heavens and a new earth in which righteousness dwells."[38]

The gift of God's righteousness in Christ to the world now is not like making a final payment. It is more like opening an account on which travelers can draw as they spend their life in a country far from home. They live in trust that the notes are good. Only in the end will they know whether the notes have been backed by gold. Meanwhile, they spend the notes with reckless confidence—putting faith in the One who has signed the notes with his life and death. It is not a blind trust. Their "hope against hope" does not curve in upon itself but is based on the reality of Christ, who is both *extra nos* and *pro nobis*. Luther's formula was *peccator in re, iustus in spe*. The gift of righteousness now announces a goal that is still future. The person who thinks he has already crossed that goal, who has already arrived, is claiming that the fullness of the future has already exhausted itself in the forms of his present. This leads to perfectionist boasting in religion and morality, generating hypocrisy and self-deception. That forgets that the coming Christ is still the final judge. No amount of religion and morality can climb onto the throne of judgment. The forensic concept of justification—if transposed into the categories of proleptic eschatology—maintains the truth of a continuing tension between the presence of divine righteousness under the signs of promise and hope and its future fulfillment in the consummation of all things.

The critical function of the message of God's righteousness is grounded in the futurity of his kingdom in relation to every present, whether the individual's, the church's, or the world's. It reveals the present under the light of God's "No." It is a searing and searching light. The "No" is directed at everything striving in enmity against "the magnificent future God has planned for us."[39] It reveals the powers gripping the world in a conspiracy to keep it the way it is. God's righteousness reveals the world as in need of a new Lord. The resurrection of Jesus is his enthronement by God to lordship. For the world this means a chance for change, a new leadership, a new loyalty, a new goal. For us as individuals it means to let the rule of God's righteousness create a new obedience in our bodies and a new loyalty in our minds. For the church it means new tongues and a new song, to proclaim to the world the news of its freedom and reconciliation, and to celebrate right now the joy of life that has burst in upon us. And so, on account of Christ, we hear the decision of God's "Yes," his acceptance of the unacceptable, his justification of the unjust, of sinners, and the godless. What does this mean for the individual person? It means that he has no illusions about himself, that he need not have any. He is *peccator in re, iustus in spe*. He confesses daily his status as a sinner, his unbelief, and godlessness. This is not degrading. He derives dignity from it by letting his sin be defined by his hope. His is not a hope-less confession. He daily seeks to be renewed in the life of hope and trust, in openness for the coming of God each day under new conditions. Every day is a new departure into

the future of God's creative love. In accepting the alien righteousness of Christ, he lets that suffice for his own future, and in this
he finds freedom to live for others. The gift of God's righteousness obligates us to the Giver; but God receives our service of
righteousness only as we pour it through the world into him.
There are no religious good works, no meritorious deeds, which
can be done directly for God. God receives our gifts only when
the world receives them first. We can mediate our love to God,
and thus be a likeness of Christ, only by holding the future open
for the hopeless of the earth and representing to them in word
and deed the new hope of mankind which was born from the
grave.

4.   AN ESCHATOLOGICAL CONCEPT
OF THE TRINITY

The presence of God's future in Jesus of Nazareth and
through his Spirit in the church offers the basis of an eschatological
concept of the tri-unity of God. The root of the doctrine of the
Trinity is God's self-definition in the person of Jesus and the sending of his Spirit. The view which sees the Trinity stretched over
the three modes of time, so widespread in ecumenical and church
publications, has done untold damage to the doctrine of God. God
the Father is then viewed as the Creator of the world in the primordial past; God the Son as the Redeemer of the world in the
midpoint of history; God the Spirit as the Sanctifier who works to
make the pious more pious. This schema can be shattered already
by Augustine's principle: *opera trinitatis ad extra indivisa sunt.*
More important, however, is its lack of solid biblical footing. Paul
Tillich appealed for a "reopening of the trinitarian problem."[40]
This should be done within the horizon of an eschatological concept of the power and presence of God's future in relation to the
world. In the first place, it calls for a new orientation of the doctrine of creation toward its goal in the kingdom of God whose

universality and futurity Jesus announced and anticipated in his own being and love for the world. The traditional Christian doctrine of creation has languished in the limbo of natural theology. Even worse, it has lingered in the shadows of the mythical Creator-God, who once upon a time created a perfect world that has been going downhill ever since.

The God who created "in the beginning" is not antecedent to the world, progressively being left behind in the primordial past as the world goes forward. He is precedent to the world as its original future, so that the beginning of the world occurs from the power of its end. What is needed to rescue the Christian doctrine of creation from its captivity to archetypal mythology and natural theology is an eschatology of creation that starts with Jesus' proclamation of the coming kingdom of God and its initial arrival (the firstfruits) in the new creation of his resurrection life. "Creation is not a protological myth of origin, but an eschatological 'project.' "[41] In pagan mythology, and to a great extent in the traditional idea of creation, the protological origin determines the measure of the future. In an eschatologically revised doctrine of creation the rule of the past is broken. The *archē* has no privilege of dominion over the creative rights of the *eschaton*. The power of the future is free to create new things, which have not been scheduled from the beginning in the primeval origins. Eschatology can free the mind of the church from its bondage to the idea that the past has to provide precedents for what the creative Spirit of the future intends to release into the present. The *eschata* of the future are not an echo of the *prōta*. The concept of an ontological circle in which the end curls back on the origin is an item of pagan mythology that has left a deep mark on the Christian doctrine of creation. Its effects still remain on the linear revision of *Heilsgeschichte* theology,[42] which views the end as a projection of the beginning, that is, as a remodeling job on an old construction that dates back to a time before the fall. Then the future of history takes its sights from an original state from which life has devolved.

The starting point for a Christian doctrine of the world as creation is not the account of its genesis in Genesis; rather it is the account of its neogenesis in the arrival of God's creative future in the resurrection of Jesus—the prolepsis of the new creation. The leitmotif of the Christian interest in creation is not that of tracing the world back to its "first cause" by the backpedaling logic of inferential reasoning. Faith in God the Creator has to do with the future of the world, its orientation to God as its goal. The confession of the world as creation arises within the horizon of God's promise which sets the world in motion toward its fulfillment. The *creatio ex nihilo* is put forth as the first miracle in light of the new creation of life from the dead. The Creator God is the God of promise "who gives life to the dead and calls into existence the things that do not exist."[43] It cannot be stressed enough that the doctrine of creation is not a piece of self-evident natural theology, to which we then have to add more problematic doctrines like resurrection or incarnation. The idea that something is created from nothing is not easier or more natural to believe than that new life is given to the dead. Creation is the world in motion toward its fulfillment in the coming *eschaton*. The *eschaton* is the creative power, the inner dynamic, of the world in process, of the history of mankind toward its integration in the lordship of Christ, and of each individual on the way to fulfillment. The propensity of creation is determined and revealed from its end in Christ. What something really is, its innermost essence, is decided by the direction in which it moves. What is true and real in a particular thing is decided by what comes out of it. "Creation is occurring from its end."[44]

The cosmic christology of the New Testament places the whole creation in relation to Christ as its agent and medium, its unity and goal.[45] The meaning of Christ is not exhausted in the issues of sin and salvation, or in the sphere of personal religion and church life. Especially today, on the mission fields and the younger churches, the "pleromatic christology"[46] of the later Paulinism in the New Testament is acquiring a renewed relevance. However, to safeguard this christology from lapsing into nature mysticism it is essential to keep it firmly within its eschatologico-historical framework. Christology provides the norm of theology, eschatology its form. This applies not only to soteriology but as well to a Christian doctrine of the world as creation—history, society, and nature. All things (*ta panta*) are oriented to the *eschaton* which has appeared in proleptic form in Jesus of Nazareth and which draws all things into the *pleroma* of the glory of God. The confession that Jesus Christ is the Lord of history and the Mediator of creation is based on the eschatological character of the Christ-event. In this event God as the power of the future has revealed himself as creative love. Out of this love he has given to each thing its measure of being, to each event its time, to each person his place, and to all things a promise of their fulfillment in the kingdom of fullness, freedom, and righteousness. Love is the ultimate ground of unity in the creative, redemptive, and consummating work of God.

The essential unity of God with Jesus of Nazareth is manifest in his absolute love, his unlimited devotion, to God as his Father and the representation of the Father's love to the world. In this is rooted the confession of the "homoousios" of the Son with the Father. The Son is doing his Father's business in the world. When God reveals himself in Jesus of Nazareth as his Son, and we confess him as our Lord, what is being witnessed is that the medium, content, and author of revelation are one and equal. When God defines himself in Jesus of Nazareth, he puts himself into the definition—kenotically—so that the finite presence of the man Jesus is capable of bearing the infinite reality and meaning of God's eschatological future. *Finitum capax infiniti*. The present can be a prolepsis of the future in that the unconditional righteousness and love of the kingdom were mediated into the world through Jesus. Through this medium God is present as the One who is future.

If we stop here we have a binitarian conception of God. There are evidences that such a view coexisted with unitarian and trinitarian conceptions for some time in the early church, until the trinitarian conception won out against both its rivals. What is at stake here is not the magical power of the number "three."[47] The Holy Spirit was experienced in the early church as the presence of the power of the future which had appeared in Jesus of Nazareth. It was not some other reality that was making itself known. The Holy Spirit was the Spirit of Christ, the risen Lord Jesus. In the Old Testament and in primitive Christianity the outpouring of the Spirit was expected as an eschatological event.[48] The Spirit is the surging power of new life and wisdom. When Jesus began reading from the prophet Isaiah, "The Spirit of the Lord is upon me," he went on to associate this with the dawning of the kingdom of God.[49] The Apostle Paul saw the Spirit as the power of God raising Jesus from the dead. Wherever men confess Jesus as Lord, there the Spirit is active. Everywhere in the New Testament the Spirit is known by his christological good works. *Kyrios* and *Pneuma* belong so closely together that Paul can even say, "Now the Lord is the Spirit, and where the Spirit of the Lord is, there is freedom."[50] It is the Spirit who calls and keeps believers in the eschatological community of Christ. "All who are led by the Spirit of God are sons of God."[51]

The Spirit is as the Spirit does. He does what the Father and the Son do. As the Son does the will of the Father, so the Spirit does the will of the Father and the Son. It is the merit of the *filioque* clause, "who proceedeth from the Father *and the Son,*" to underscore the christological norm in any theology of the Holy Spirit. There can be no spiritual presence worthy of the name Christian which does not mediate the future of God exclusively through the Christ of hope. Because Christ is one with God, the Spirit he sends as his indwelling presence in believers is also "homoousios" with God the Father. The Spirit is the power of unity, integrating believers with each other in the body of Christ and binding them with Christ to God the Father. He can do the work of unity because he is originally the power of unity in the reciprocating relation between the Father and the Son. The vitalities of faith, hope, and love in the church and the world proceed from the Spirit of the new reality that arrived in Jesus of Nazareth and his resurrection from the dead. The doctrine of the Spirit has its essential foundation in the appearance of the risen Jesus to his disciples. As the disciples "see" Jesus, he sends them and gives them the Holy Spirit.[52] The Spirit is after that the driving power of the mission of hope to the nations.

The doctrine of the Trinity is, thus, the most adequate interpretation of the eschatological structure of God's self-revelation in Jesus of Nazareth and in the Spirit who creates a community of believers who already participate through hope in the future of God, and thus exist toward the future as the proleptic sign and sacrament of a new world. In saying this we dispense with all speculations about a Trinity as he is in himself apart from his self-revelation as the living God in Jesus and his Spirit. Discussion of the Trinity in abstraction from the proleptic presence of the future of God in Jesus of Nazareth and his outgoing Spirit make it an object of superstitious adoration or, as Tillich said, "the riddle of an unsolved theological problem . . . the glorification of an absurdity in numbers."[53] That the doctrine of the Trinity was no such thing to the fathers of the ancient church who fully developed its final orthodox form is clear from the christological starting point of the trinitarian controversy. However, the mere recitation of their fixed formulae, as much as that may be justified in the worship of the church, does not offer a key to open up what they saw in the doctrine of the Trinity. Frequently in church history the issue at stake in trinitarian controversy has been obedience to the authority of the church and its creedal norms. The church can no longer hold on to the doctrine of the Trinity for the sake of tradition or expect assent to it out of deference to ecclesiastical authority. The church is badly in need of a key by which to unlock the treasury of meaning that once was cached in its doctrine of the Trinity. Here we suggest that the right key is the presence of God's ultimate future in the man Jesus of Nazareth. The doctrine of the Trinity describes the identity of God's future under the different modes of his appearance to the world.[54] The unity of God and the trinitarian distinctions can be explicated best on the basis of the one future of God that has entered into the person of Jesus and the Spirit of life he sends into the world to create faith, hope, and love. Speculations about the inner-trinitarian relations in the eternal being of God are valid only if they deepen our understanding of the eschatological content of revelation through history. If they lead our attention away from the historical medium of revelation to some eternally preexisting hinterland, they conflict with the christological norm of theology— *was Christum treibt.* On the ground of the unity of being and act in the process of God's self-revelation in Jesus of Nazareth, we may hold that God is as God does, that he is the way he reveals himself, that the trinitarian differentiation of his unity in the Christ-event is grounded in the inner self-determination of God as Father-Son-Spirit.

FOUR

The Prolepsis of
a New World - Church

1. THE KINGDOM OF GOD AND THE CHURCH

It is widely acknowledged that for the New Testament the church is an eschatological event. This means that the kingdom of God is the point of departure for understanding what the church is.[1] The church cannot reach a proper understanding of itself and of its function in the world by dwelling on itself. The church is really an eschatological community of hope that exists for the world. An adequate definition of the church must build the eschatological hope for the world's future into its center. Such a definition must take seriously the church's primary function to proclaim and pioneer the future of the world within the horizon of faith in God's coming kingdom. As a start we shall define the church as the prolepsis of a new world that is coming into being through the power of God's creative future in Christ. The church as a new community of hope has been founded by the impact of the future of God in the history of Jesus, in his cross and resurrection. The eschatological character of this event exerted an attracting power on all sorts and conditions of men, gathering them from out of all nations into a new and really the first and only true international community, existing as a sign of hope for the future of mankind.

The church is constituted as a mission of hope to the nations. The church does not exist *from* itself and *for* itself. Ecclesiocentricity is the primal sin of the new people of God. The church exists *from* the kingdom of God which Jesus proclaimed and embodied in his own person and ministry; and it exists *for* the world for which Jesus died and was raised again. The concern for the world is not an extracurricular activity. Rather, the kingdom of God toward which the church is striving embraces the future of the whole world. The idea of the kingdom of God cannot be thought at all without including in it the element of universality. If the kingdom of God is the promised future of the church, it is no less the future of the world. The church is the place where the world has become conscious of its future destiny in the kingdom of God's freedom and love. The church should cease thinking of itself as nonworld, as antithetical to the world. For what the church already enjoys is a sign of what the world still has in store for it. The church exists ahead of the world as the bearer of signs and promises that reach out to encompass the totality of reality.

If the church at any period of its history must brace itself in opposition to the world, this is a posture which must be justified in light of its real mission to the world. It must not become a permanent state of mind. On the other hand, when the relations of the church to the world are harmonious, the church must ask whether this concordat of peace has been achieved by conforming to the world. For the church to conform to the world is to fall back to where it once was, to be out of joint with the new time of day. A period of smooth relations with the world might call for a revolutionary initiative by the church to become the protagonist of the voiceless in society, and thus fulfill its role as the fighting agent of God's rule in history. The church can neither separate

itself from the world nor merge with it. It cannot separate from
the world, because the kingdom of God which has become proleptically present in Jesus of Nazareth is the true future of both
the church and the world. It cannot merge with the world, because then it would lose its distinctive calling to keep the fires of
hope burning in history for the fulfillment of individuals, of humanity, and of the cosmos, in the absolute future of God. Because
the church exists to serve the kingdom of God in history, it is
pointed toward the world, as light to the nations, as the new mankind foreshadowing the future of universal humanity in Jesus the
Messiah—the Omega point of the history of reality. The fidelity
of the church to its Lord is expressed in its vital consciousness of
bearing the good news of a new world, of hopeful destiny and
ultimate fulfillment for the reality of history en route to the future.
Any dimming of this eschatological consciousness results in the
relaxation of the church's missionary existence for the world.

The eschatological horizon of the church, embracing the
whole world, is what keeps it from identifying itself with the
kingdom of God and turning in upon itself in spiritual ecclesiocentricity. The church is not the kingdom of God, but only the
sacramental sign of the new world that is emerging in, with, and
under the manifestations of the present, visible world. The church
is on the way; it has not yet reached the goal of hope. And at
last when the kingdom of God has fully come and the world has
reached its transcendent destiny in the future of God, there will
be no church. The church, however, exists now as the chosen instrument of God's rule for the sake of the world. If the church
understands itself as God's eschatological mission for the world,
it will not think of itself as a group of individuals who withdraw
from the world to satisfy one another's emotional needs. The
sight of a congregation gathering on Sunday morning to let off
some spiritual steam or for emotional therapy is a common betrayal
of the church's basic orientation to the kingdom of God and to
the world. When the church is preoccupied with filling its own

religious needs, the gates of the kingdom are closed to it. For the gates of the kingdom are open to the church only as the church is open to the world. Moreover, the church is fast losing out as an emotional crutch in modern society.

It is common for Christians in the Reformation tradition to define the church as "the congregation of saints, in which the Gospel is rightly taught and the Sacraments are rightly administered."[2] This is a partial definition. But what is left out of the definition is as important as what is included. There is no mention here of the eschatological basis of the church in the kingdom of God and of the missionary function of the church in world history. Therefore, the unending recitation of this definition has done nothing to combat the deeply ingrown ecclesiocentric habit of thought and action in the church's history.[3] This definition of the church does not swing between the poles of the kingdom of God and of the world. So it might seem that the church is a group of people who get together to hear the gospel and receive the sacraments. Of course, that is true, but such a getting together, such hearing and receiving, can be authentically Christian only within the horizon of an eschatological vision of a new world in the future of God's rule. The omission of explicit reference to the eschatological and missionary dimensions of the church's essence has permitted a series of blunders to occur in Protestantism: the rejection of world mission in the period of Orthodoxy, the "little flock" mentality of Pietism, the quietistic attitude toward the social and political crises in modern times, and in general a dualistic view of the church's relation to the world.

It would seem, then, that the image of the church as the getting together of saints (*congregatio sanctorum*) is neither deep enough nor broad enough. The starting point for a definition of the church is only deep enough when it begins with the message of the kingdom of God, and only broad enough when it comprehends the world as the field of its mission. It is this mission which constitutes the nature of the church. We cannot first define the nature of the church, then tack on its mission as optional activity. The *esse* of the church is to exist as a function of the kingdom of God in the open field of world history.

In both Roman Catholic and Protestant theology there is an earnest search for the appropriate point of departure for a doctrine of the church. The ancient church endured centuries of conflict over christology, the medieval church over sacramentology, the Reformation over soteriology. It has fallen to the modern church to have its fundamental problem focus on ecclesiology. It is rather surprising that it has taken the church twenty centuries to come around to the question of a true definition concerning itself. The doctrine of the church is one of the most underdeveloped areas in the history of Christian thought. There is no orthodox dogma on the church in the classical Christian tradition which can claim to be authoritative. The mention of the church in the ecumenical creeds was not motivated by polemical intent. The formula *una sancta catholica et apostolica* was not ever contested by any heretical party in the ancient church. And there is no denomination or sect in modern Christianity that is inclined to contest the formula as such. It is only when we strive to reach a dogmatically precise ecclesiology that controversial issues supervene. Up to Vatican II many people imagined that if anywhere there existed an amply developed concept of the church, it was in Roman Catholic theology. Since the convening of the council the opposite has proved true. The degree of sheer flux and the liveliness of the debate on the doctrine of the church in Roman Catholicism have been both astonishing and promising. It would be rather pathetic if Protestants would remain immobilized by a sixteenth-century congregationalist definition of the church at a time when Roman Catholics are freeing themselves from a rigidly hierarchical and monarchical view of the church. Both sides have to profit by vastly improved methods of biblical inquiry, a broader knowledge of the whole sweep of the Christian tradition in East and West, and the challenges of the modern world to create new structures for the church's life and mission.

In the nineteenth century, Roman Catholic theology thought of the church as the kingdom of God. Even in some circles of Protestant thought there was a virtual identification of the church with the kingdom of God. Prayer for the coming of God's kingdom was thought of in terms of spreading the church's influence, or as *ecclesia plantanda*. Church work was promoted purely and simply as building up the kingdom. Full-time church workers enjoyed a rank above others. The rediscovery of eschatology though the studies of Johannes Weiss and Albert Schweitzer and those since has demonstrated the error of identifying the church with the kingdom of God. As the New Testament understands it, the kingdom of God is the supreme power of God's universal rule, not an ecclesiastical society on earth with its own hierarchical structure, modeled after the Roman Empire or the sovereign states of Western Europe. What was right in this nineteenth-century view was the idea that the church can be properly defined only in terms of the kingdom of God. What was wrong was, first, the supplanting of the eschatological by a sociological view of the kingdom and, second, the identification of the church with the kingdom. The recovery of the eschatological horizon makes the identification no longer possible.

In the search for a new concept of the church, the impact of Pauline studies advanced the image of the "body of Christ" to the fore. Especially in Roman Catholic and Anglican theology the "body of Christ" concept was made the starting point of the doctrine of the church. As Gustave Weigel stated: "The result was a war between those who used the kingdom of God concept and those who replaced it with the notion of the *soma tou Christou*."[4] It is obvious that in this war Weigel allied himself with those who stressed the organic symbolism of the body rather than the political symbol of the kingdom. When Weigel was writing in America in the early sixties, he gave the impression that the most up-to-date Roman theologians were all on the side of the "body of Christ" as the leading ecclesiological motif. Meanwhile in Europe quite a different motif was beginning to gain ground, the idea of the church as the *laos tou theou*. Although Weigel made the claim that "ecclesiology is my own specialization,"[5] he did not breathe a word about the new trend in Roman Catholic circles to think of the church as the people of God.[6] The fact that he was apparently unaware of this development is a sign of how quickly theological fashions have been changing in the Roman Catholic Church. Rival ecclesiologies can be built on the quite dissimilar images of the church as "kingdom of God" or "body of Christ" or "people of God."

Something ironical, however, has been happening. At the very time that Roman theology was moving away from the "kingdom of God" concept as the right starting point for its doctrine of the church, Protestant theology was returning to it under the impact of the modern rediscovery of eschatology. Even the "people of God" concept cannot stand by itself. It needs the eschatological basis in the kingdom of God to counteract the suggestion that the church might be a chosen people as an end in itself. God did not choose a people on whom to lavish special privileges. He chose a people as a provisional instrument to proclaim and pioneer the future of the entire history of creation. He called the church to serve as a prolepsis of the new world that lies within the potential of his creative intention. Starting with the kingdom of God as the basis of the church, it is essential to drive through the world to the kingdom of God. There is no relation between the kingdom of God and the church that does not intersect the world. There is no way of serving God without serving the world. God in himself has no need of our service, only his world does. The vocation of the church under the kingdom of God is to pave the way for the future of mankind. A church that is in arrears of the world with

respect to the new things which God is creating through history
is a scandalous betrayal of its eschatological charter.

The kingdom of God concept can help the church to purge
itself of its church-centered thinking and to renew its commitment
to the world without taking the easy course proposed by the advocates of secular Christianity. Secular Christianity only gives to the
world what it already has; it tells the world what it already knows.
Secular Christianity is filled with the guilt of Christendom's
arrogant triumphalist past. To relieve its guilt pangs it is willing
to go to bed with the world on any terms which the world is
pleased to dictate. Toward the end of the nineteenth century a
Protestant pastor in an industrial city in Germany, who was in-
fluenced by Marxist ideas, prophesied the advent of a "secularized
Christianity in the future."[7] Today this prophecy is coming true.
The name of the prophet was Albert Kalthoff (1850–1906). He
was able to match any of the absurdities uttered by the so-called
radicals of today. He denied that Jesus ever existed on earth, and
he discarded the idea of the living God of the Bible. The "new
essence of Christianity" which he envisioned was a syndrome of
revolutionary forces and communist ideals at work in the interest
of the oppresed masses and the struggling proletariat. Jesus Christ
was for him the mythical personification of the aspirations of the
impoverished masses. The way to empty the Christian message of
its distinctive content has not changed since Kalthoff's day, that
is, to cut the artery of life that leads from God's eschatological
future into the world through the history of Jesus of Nazareth. It
is this eschatological message which prevents the church from in-
flating itself at the world's expense, but which also guards it
against the false self-deflation in secular Christianity.

2.   PROLEPTIC SIGNS OF THE NEW WORLD

Perhaps the majority of people in our society think of the
church as one of the last bastions of the old world. The church
looks like a medieval cathedral and smells like a museum. And

that is why many people still bother with the church. It gives them a handle on the old world to which they long to return. The good old days of Christendom are something to dream about. The church is seen as an island of refuge from the maelstrom of change in the modern world. Those who cannot stand the bad weather outside may enter the sheltering asylum of the church. The church is full of refugees from the dizzying cycles of change in society. Consequently many Christians have difficulty associating the church with change. In their heart they side with those Jews who brought the accusation before the city authorities of Thessalonica concerning the preaching of Paul and Silas: "These men have turned the world upside down."[8]

The church is not a paradise of changelessness. "For here we have no lasting city, but we seek the city which is to come."[9] The church is true to its inner eschatological dynamic when it gives exuberant expression to its passion for the future. For the church is the primary sacrament of the new world of the future. The church is not a monument erected in remembrance of a bygone world. It is not a society of emigrés who get together in foreign lands to preserve their old ways and customs. The new world of the future is present in the church so far as it is a sacramental anticipation of the kingdom of God. The church is an expedition on the way to explore the future; it is not a pilgrimage to revisit all the sacred sites of the past. The function of memory is to serve hope, the function of tradition to send forth signals of promise of what is on the way toward us. The church has attained no lasting form. The consciousness of its own destiny reminds the church of its merely provisional character. The church will be surpassed by the new heaven and the new earth that its message announces to the world. One day the church as church will become obsolete when God arrives in the fullness of his glory to bring the world home to its future identity in him. Meanwhile the church exists to exhibit through its life *in* the world a living hope *for* the world.

The church is set in the world as the firstfruits of the new creation.[10] The term "firstfruits" in the New Testament is applied first of all to the resurrected Christ: He is the firstfruits of those who are raised to the newness of life.[11] But the very same term is applied to the church: We are the firstfruits of God's creatures, the firstfruits of the Spirit, who await the fullness of life on the basis of the promising action of God in raising Jesus from the dead. As the firstfruits the church is a sign, a pledge, a beginning of the new world that is being mediated by God's historical activity. It is false for the church to think that it has already arrived, and that the ultimate blessing for the world is to join the church.

The church is the place where the shape of the future is being prefigured and proleptically realized through the eschatological word of grace and salvation. The Spirit of Christ makes the eschatological word of the future a vital reality in the present life of faith. This is what it means to bind the life of the church on earth to the word and sacraments. The eschatological existence of the church in the world means to live already from the coming future. Then we can be free in the present situation and remember our past with joy. The eschatological word makes the new world already sacramentally present. "When anyone is united to Christ, there is a new world; the old order has gone, and a new order has already begun."[12] The word makes the old too small to contain our hopes. Change is needed to make room for new things. The preaching of the church has to be from first to last an eschatological act which brings the new future into our historical situation. The word is a sacrament of the eschatological future because it brings what it proclaims. The basic axiom of sacramentology is that a sacrament does what it says and says what it does. *Sacramenta efficiunt quod significant et significant quod efficiunt.*[13] A sacramental sign or symbol participates in the reality to which it points.[14] The word of preaching is sacramental because it creates a real presence of the future within us, so far as truth and love and peace and freedom—the gifts of the Spirit—begin to hold sway among us.

The crisis in modern Christianity can be traced to the sterility of its word of preaching. The word of the gospel is meant to be good news of the kingdom. But why is the preaching of the church so boring and stale, both to those who hear and to those who preach? It is bound to be boring if it does not relate to reality, and it will be stale if it does not bring the newness of the future into history. The preaching of the church which does not arise out of the tension between the future of God's kingdom and the present reality of this world is lacking its New Testament credentials. Preaching is interesting when the proleptic word of God's future attacks the roots of negativity in the present. This is preaching as law. Its target is sin—any power which keeps the reality of the world from catching up with the future of Christ. Christ is the world's forerunner, leading the procession of world history into the open space of God's freedom and fulfilling love. If preaching is understood eschatologically, the word will open up the distance and the difference between the present of the world and its future in God's kingdom. This word will be heard as a call for the world to change, to be transformed into the new reality of the future. Only in the resurrection of Jesus, so far as we know, has the word of God's eschatological future reached a moment of identity with existing reality. Everything else in the world is destined to change before it reaches its homeland of identity in the fullness of God. The eschatological word brings a foretaste of the future. This is preaching as gospel. The word is a two-edged sword—law and gospel. As law the word attacks everything in the present that refuses to inherit the future; as gospel the word brings samples of the ultimate future into the pain of the present. The word is not adequately understood as information about the past or as meditation on the present. It is the call of the future into the present, announcing what must yet happen to bring the reality of the world into agreement with the word of God's promise. The word is not primarily true doctrine or existential address. It is the verbal prolepsis of the new world,[15] and therefore the driving wedge of the power of God's future in the depths of existence and the processes of history. If preaching is understood as the action of the eschatological word in history, it will create an atmosphere of interest in new things and hope for a new world, a new humanity, a new creation. The living word brings the future of life so near that we can already taste it. Thus faith in the word of promise is a foretaste of that life and light and love that will be fully revealed and realized at the end.

Holy Communion is a sacrament of the kingdom of God in the world. It is not a purely churchly affair. The Supper is a miniature meal eaten together in anticipation of the messianic banquet. The eschatological banquet of the Messiah is for all the nations. Holy Communion is a prolepsis of the final rendezvous of all the separated in the world to come. The broken and disrupted relations between men are being healed in the koinonia of the Lord. The Lord invites to Holy Communion the many in order to make them one. He welcomes those from the East and the West, the North and the South, the poor and the rich, radicals and reactionaries, the slaves and the free, the Brahmins and the Pariahs, Black Power people and Ku Klux Klanners. He calls sinners, and not the righteous, into his forgiving fellowship. In Holy Communion those things which divide us are taken up into the body of Christ. Reconciliation happens. As whites and blacks break bread together, they are doing in the name of Christ a most humanly intimate thing which is bound to trigger off a chain reaction of revolutionary impulses through the body of society. Those who eat and drink together in church, sharing a common joy and hope, will never be satisfied in a society that lags behind this communal experience.

If Holy Communion is the sacrament of the kingdom of God, a kind of prerepresentation of the messianic future in history, its liturgy must sound forth the note of joy. Those who work at liturgical renewal would do an important thing if they would recapture the dimension of eschatological joy in our worship. True enough, joy is not the only aspect of the eucharistic celebration; it is only the most neglected one. When we celebrate Holy Communion, we remember the death of Jesus on the cross. A sepulchral and penitential mood sweeps over the congregation. This is not right. Our remembrance of the death of Jesus is not meant to create funereal feelings. The memorial aspect is set within the horizon of eschatological expectation. When we eat and drink together, we are proclaiming the Lord's death "until he comes."[16] The primitive Aramaic prayer *Marana tha,* "Our Lord, come," expresses the nucleus of the eschatological outlook of the early Christian eucharists. Schweitzer went so far as to say: "What constitutes the essential character of the early Christian meal is . . . *wholly* and *solely* in the petition and thanksgiving for the Coming of the Kingdom."[17] At the Last Supper, Jesus himself struck the eschatological note by declaring: "I shall not drink again of the fruit of the vine until that day when I drink it new in the kingdom of God."[18]

The eschatological perspective means that our Lord's Supper is not a mere memorial of the Last Supper. That would be the right and fitting thing to do if ours were a dead Christ. Then gloom and not joy would be called for. When Christians gather to eat and to drink, they are not playing at being disciples in the Upper Room. Time is not canceled backward so that they can reenact the historical drama of that last meal with Jesus. Then we should be understandably sorrowful at the thought of having to part with our Master. Instead, our remembrance of Jesus arouses expectant joy because he was raised to be the Lord of the future. In Holy Communion we declare that we are leaving the old world behind in joyful anticipation of the new. What we celebrate is the birth of newness, the new life in Christ, the presence of the Spirit as the guarantee of the promised goal, and the vision of the new world that is coming to man. Joy is the offspring of hope, nourished by the promise of the future of life for our bodies and a righteousness that rules forever. We should let the joy of our hope find new ways to celebrate the coming of the new world in new songs and in new tongues. The liturgies of Christians should be miniature miracles of Pentecost on the way to perfect joy and love in the new world to come. Especially the liturgy of Holy Communion should be a sacrament of joy and thanksgiving, for here the church partakes, as it were, ahead of time of the eschatological feast that is spread by the victorious Host of the new world in the kingdom of God. The glory of the approaching kingdom, its beauty and incomprehensible richness, should be prefigured and foreshown by our songs of mirth and gladness. We celebrate the joy that came to the world through "the death of death" and "the annihilation of hell."[19] The ascetic spirit which rids worship of things to see and hear and smell and touch and taste is a curse on the Protestant tradition. Is is a curse, however, which cannot be removed by going back, by fiddling around with gambits and gimmicks which liturgical hobbyists dig out of the old manuals of worship. The search for new forms should be guided by the eschatological forces that are embryonically present in the gospel of the kingdom of God. Then mere past precedents will not justify present actions. The prejudice that something is better if it is old is fine only for antique collectors. From the beginning, Christianity has been in quest of a new cult for the newness of the gospel. Imagine what a change was required to shift the Sabbath from Saturday to Sunday, for baptism to replace circumcision, for the Lord's Supper to replace the Passover, for the smoke of sacrifice curling heavenward to be exchanged for the confession of a contrite heart, for those of heathen and Gentile birth to become naturalized citizens of the kingdom of God. The freedom to innovate is manifestly the birthright of the eschatological community that lives toward the future of God's kingdom.

Holy Baptism is also an eschatological sacrament in the situation between the old world and the new. The eschatological horizon is clear from the contrast between the baptism of John and Christian baptism. John baptized with water unto repentance.

The Spirit and the fire that are added in Christian baptism reveal its eschatological character. Baptism is an act of putting off the old and taking on the new. It is founded on the death and resurrection of the Messiah Jesus. Baptism involves the individual in the drama of the shifting of the aeons. This is best symbolized through baptism by immersion. When the individual goes under the water, he is assigning an end to the rule of sin, death, and the devil in his life. When he comes up, he turns his back on the old and faces the future with a new loyalty. He is now in a situation of no longer having to sin (*posse non peccare*).[20] The person, however, who claims to be already sinless as a matter of fact (i. e., *iustus in re*) is overlooking the difference between eschatological existence in the present and existence in the eschatological future. Even Paul confessed that he had not already obtained and was not already perfect, but that he still had to press on toward a goal that lies in the future.[21] Baptism stands at the beginning of a daily struggle against the old for the sake of walking in the newness of life.[22]

Prayer is the language of hope for the coming of God's kingdom. The familiar praying posture of eyes closed, hands folded, and knees bent is a mystical model that is no fundamental part of the Christian idea of prayer. Today's praying will likely take a different form, less interiorized and more open to the world around. Leslie Dewart's suggestion might have some shock value also for our thinking about prayer in the modern world: "I think that the Christian theism of the future might so conceive God as to find it possible to look back with amusement on the day when it was thought particularly appropriate that the believer should bend his knee in order to worship God. For when the eyes of the Christian faith remove their hellenic lenses, what continues to appear sacred about hierarchical relations as such?"[23] Prayer does not let God in by closing out the world. Prayer is a call to God to keep the promises he has made to his people for the world. In prayer we hold the unredeemed face of this world up to the picture of God's promised future, and wrestle with him in the agony of the contradiction. The world is not yet what it ought to be, not yet what God has promised to make it in the future of his kingdom. Prayer is the groaning of the soul: "How long, O Lord, how long?"[24] The "Amen" of prayer is the assurance of faith that God will be true to his word. Because God delivered his word to the world in the name of Jesus, Christians name that name in summoning God to remember the world according to the generosity of his promise.

3.   THE RELATIVITY OF THE STRUCTURES

The eschatological word of the gospel is the basis of the unity of Scripture and the continuity of the Christian tradition. The structures of the church and its tradition transmit a message whose eschatological character relativizes all the structures. Nothing in and of the church can be exempt from the criticism that emanates from the eschatological word of God's future in the Christ-event. The reality of the eschatological future is proleptically manifest in the christological foundation of the church. The church in history meets every new situation with reference to that future which has already been previewed in the coming of the crucified and risen Lord. The anticipation of this future reacts upon the church's traditional structures, and puts a question to them whether they can still serve as signs and instruments of the new world of Christ. The fact that a structure can be traced back to the ancient church, or even to the Bible, is no sufficient reason to keep it. The authority of the Scripture itself cannot be based on its antiquity or on the tradition of the church. The authority of any structure of tradition derives from the eschatological root of the gospel in the appearance of Jesus Christ. That is what it means to speak with Luther of *was Christum treibt* as the norm of truth.

The confessions and doctrines of the church are not their

own authority. The sheer variety of contradictory beliefs about what Christian faith really is invalidates a positivistic attitude toward the traditions of the church. Christianity is not everything that calls itself Christian, any more than calling oneself a Buddhist would make it so. The quest for the essence and continuing identity of Christianity in history zeroes in upon the Scriptures as the witness to the union of the eschatological future with the historical event of Jesus Christ. The unity of the eschatological and historical dimensions of this event establishes the unity of Scripture, the unity of the church, and the continuing identity of its essential life in, with, and under the new traditions which are now being created. The Bible has the primacy over every other norm in the church because the light of God's future has fallen upon it most clearly. Every tradition or doctrine of the church must be tested in that light by every new generation of Christians. Even the best formulations of the past are subject to the eschatological provision in the Christ-event that founded the church. This renders all past and present structures of the tradition provisional and relative. Does this place them at the mercy of the subjectivity of modern man? Not at all, for the norms of modernity are subject to the same eschatological proviso. The eschatological truth of revelation is now at best available to us in forms of doctrine and life that share in the relativities of the historical process. We know only in part. The treasures of truth come to us in vessels of clay. The difference between the proleptic form of the truth and its final fullness will never be overcome as long as the church is on its pilgrim way. It is the task of church dogmatics to spell out this difference, to keep the preaching of the gospel as pure as possible and to deliver the church in every age from the illusion of thinking it has reached the end of the road.

A burning eschatological consciousness will shed new light on the structural problem of the church today. This problem still looms up as the major hurdle on the way to the reunion of the churches.[25] Already pressures from biblical studies, on the one side, and from the modern world, on the other side, have softened some of the older rigidities. However, the hard core of the issue remains, and will melt away further only by the heat of the eschatological fire that is fed by the gospel of God's kingdom. Is there a definite order of the church of Jesus Christ? Is this order hierarchical in character? Is the church as the eschatological community a hierarchically constituted society? Are the traditional structures of the church, especially those most controversial ones that deal with ecclesiastical offices, episcopal succession, and papal infallibility, part of the givenness of the gospel *ab origine?* The task of theology is to find a way out of the ecumenical stalemate that has been reached on those issues.

The unity of the church cannot be achieved by scrapping the traditional structures, such as clergy and laity, or for that matter, episcopacy and papacy. The *tabula rasa* approach to ecumenical reunion is fruitlessly unrealistic. We can never build a new church from scratch. It would seem, then, that we are faced with the depressing alternative of ecumenical horse-trading, each church negotiating the best deal it can get for its own tradition. A new comprehensive structure will try to be all things to all merging groups. This is depressing, for it could all happen so beautifully without the truth of the gospel. It reminds one of the old German maxim: *"Operation glänzend gelungen. Patient leider tot."*[26] The unity of the church can be forged anew only by putting the question of the truth of the gospel ahead of the structure of the church. We must know what any church structures are for, lest the church's institutions be enemies of its world mission. Bishop Pike once quipped that while his church had apostolic succession, other churches were enjoying the apostolic success. Apostolic success at least means that evangelical truth takes priority over ecclesiastical unity. A reunited church of the future which subordinated the truth of the gospel to a form of organizational unity could easily become the throne of the anti-Christ. It is hard to see how Christians can be joined by a bond of unity that is not based on community of faith in the gospel of Christ. Ecclesiastical draftsmen can design the external appearance of unity. But genuine unity is a gift of the gospel. If it is the gospel of God's kingdom that drives us, it creates structures which express the unity we seek, not just for Christians but for the whole of mankind. The marks of the church—its unity and universality—are not static attributes but proleptic signs of the future of the world. Therefore, the structures of the church must give movement to the faith, hope, and love that have their life only by being poured out in mission to the world. The unity of the church does not rest on the ecclesiastical office, of whatever kind, but on the eschatological goal of the gospel that embraces the future of the whole world. We reach the question of the right structure of the church only by thinking from the end toward the present, from the coming of God's kingdom to its mission in the world through the church. There are no right orders which can guarantee the church. Right orders do not necessarily result in proper functions. Even in Roman Catholic theology there is no guarantee that the Pope will not fall into heresy and that bishops will not create schisms. In short, the structures are not self-authenticating. They derive their validity as church offices only so far as they serve as instruments of the gospel and signs of hope for the future of the world. We need, for example, an office that sees over (*episcopus*) the unity of the church, but only so far as it is the true unity in the gospel. This unity is not something the church can possess as an end in itself. It is a missionary unity, a provisional sign of the future unity of mankind in the kingdom of God.

The concentration on the gospel of the kingdom of God relativizes without minimizing the importance of ecclesiastical structures. The only alternative to the organized church is a disorganized one. The belittling of the institutionality of the church can be temporarily justified only as a reaction of young people to the dismal future of living in the prefabricated houses of their fathers. Since Christianity is a historical, social reality, it will always embody itself in concrete, visible structures. To talk about the unity of the church, therefore, in strictly spiritualistic terms is the heresy of Docetism in ecclesiology. The concern for a visible form of unity is a concomitant of a historical community of faith whose eschatological mission to the world is to prelude the unity for which all are destined in the future of God. If the Christian community is not visibly one in some unmistakable way, it obscures its reality as a provisional realization of the peace and unity, achieved with justice and freedom, which the world has in store for it.

There is no reason why Christians of the Reformation tradition should not be open to the possibility that when the churches reunite in the future, they will be equipped with structures that are recognizably continuous with papal and episcopal offices. I say "continuous" to emphasize that in their present form these structures are offensive on two counts. First, they function on the basis of a dogmatic that was written when the preaching of the eschatological gospel was at its lowest ebb in the church. Second, they function on the basis of an ideology which developed authoritarian features that are now anachronistic.[27] The absolutistic claims for episcopacy and papacy—not the offices as such—must wither in face of the eschatological word of the gospel. Their authoritarian aspects will necessarily be sloughed off by a "world come of age." And since Christians are modern men, they will welcome episcopal and papal structures only when they have been dedogmatized and deideologized. These structures will have to make their way in the modern world without such *a priori* claims, without any advance billing subscribed by heaven. In an un-Protestant-sounding phrase, they must be justified by works alone, and not by faith. By their fruits we will know whether they are of the gospel. They will have to take the lead in sacrificing all authoritarian features which are self-exalting and keep men down in a state of adolescent immaturity. Non-Roman Christians ought to make clear that they have no doctrinal objections to the papal and episcopal offices as such, but only to the false doctrinal claims and the exercise of authoritarian power which developed in the Roman West. The cultural situation of the past accounts for the rise of these claims and practices. But that situation exists no longer, and no Roman Catholic under forty wants to return to it. If these structures are stripped of their outdated aspects, it may be that they will serve as representative signs of the continuity of the church with Jesus and the apostles and as special agencies to care for the self-identity of the church through the discontinuities of the historical process. They may be specially concerned with the task of transmitting the best traditions of the gospel to every new generation. There will always be a need of specialized forms of ministry to the people of God in history. The special offices in the church must be transformed to catch up to modern needs and realities. As the new eschatological community in which the charismata of the Spirit are bestowed variously upon all, and in which all are ordained through their baptism to grow up to maturity, the church can set aside all authoritarian forms which diminish the vision of the new age. If the church is the representative of the kingdom of God in history, there should be political signs of the dawning of newness and freedom. There must be leadership without authoritarianism, disciplined life without coerced obedience, unity without uniformity, freedom of inquiry without blind fideism.

The ruling structures in the church have their right only as serving structures. It may be that it once seemed culturally appropriate that ecclesiastical offices should exercise ruling functions from the top down. A certain parallelism is visible between the structures that seem normal in society and the ones that arise in the church. Before one believed in the divine right of bishops or popes, one had already believed in the divine right of kings and emperors. Life in the church followed the same grain as life in society. At times the reverse might have been closer to the truth. At any rate, the structures that proved most appropriate, whether

in church or society at large, from the ancient world to the Enlightenment and the French Revolution were authoritarian in
character. Of course, at that time they were not thought of as
authoritarian. A structure seems authoritarian to those who have
had a taste of freedom. Thus, when the same structures exercise
their claims on us today, we have enough human dignity or love
of Christian freedom to revolt. This is what the authority crisis is
all about in modern Christianity, in both the Roman and the
Protestant communities. The authoritarian structures are breaking
down, and especially their claims to rule by divine right from
above, *ex sese.*

The *Constitution on the Church* of Vatican II did not succeed
in emancipating itself from its traditionally authoritarian way of
speaking "On the Hierarchy." The old Roman, juridical mind was
still in control of this chapter. It is only a question of time, however, before the death rattle will be heard in these words, especially those that pertain to the papacy. Vatican II missed the
opportunity to formulate a doctrine that followed through on the
initiative of Pope John's personal example as the servant of
servants. Roman Catholics will have to rethink their notion of
papal infallibility, and why should this be more painful than the
challenge which most Protestants have faced in abandoning the
false security of a literally inspired, infallible Bible? In an age of
historical consciousness, especially within the eschatological horizon of Christian faith, such things as infallible authorities, in-
errant writings, and absolute principles are in a bad way. What is
infallible is the fidelity of God to the future of his promise toward
which we live by the courage of hope. If we want more security
than the promise of God, we will have to exchange it for an idol
that promises instant salvation. We live by hope or we live by
sight, and there is no right way of synthesizing them. If we wish
to speak of the infallibility of the church, we must be aware that
this is very confusing shorthand for the unfailing action of God's
grace upon the church. There is no *opus operatum* which lets the

church rest upon its own endowment. The church is on the way as the pilgrim people who dare not boast of their own charm. When the Pope speaks of his own infallibility, it sounds like boasting, as though he possesses the charism of perfection. It is not understood in his own church as a very ambiguous witness to the generosity of God's grace in the life of the church. Leslie Dewart is on the right track in stating: "The doctrine of the infallibility of the magisterium of the Church, particularly in respect to the infallibility of the pope, would be misunderstood if one neglected the intrinsic reference of that infallibility to the faith of the Church. What is radically infallible is that faith. That is, we believe that the faith of the Church is privileged in that it shall not suffer ultimate failure, a privilege which, of course, no individual believer ever has . . . . Essentially, it can only be the assurance of the ultimately unfailing nature of the Christian faith in and through the establishment of a legitimate teaching authority for the benefit of the faith of the Church as a whole. The 'privilege' of infallibility is thus essentially related to the *eschatological* nature of the Church as a *believing community.*"[28] The crucial word is "eschatological." An eschatological perspective radicalizes the relativity of the church's structures, and makes it clear that infallibility cannot mean security, inerrancy, omniscience, and the like. The church travels in history under the sign of the cross, in humility and service, not in the arrogance of power and triumphal self-assertiveness. We cannot allow an ecclesiology of glory to overshadow the church's eschatology of the cross. For the glory of the risen Christ is hidden under the sign of the cross also for those who believe. If Karl Rahner is correct in his estimate that Vatican II stands at the beginning and not at the end of the road to *aggiornamento,* then we might also hope that the recovery of the eschatological impact of the gospel in the church will relativize the ecclesial structures so that the reunion of the churches might soon occur for the sake of their mission in the world. As the gospel of God's kingdom generates the unity that propels toward mission, within the Roman and Reformation traditions alike, the time will come when it will seem promiscuous to go on having such intimate relations without consummating the ecumenical love affair in marriage. The question arises how long the period of courtship needs to be in the case of the remarriage of divorced partners.

The churches must be willing to change their structures of administration and ministry more cheerfully than is apparent. The past hangs heavy on the churches, and their instinct is to cling to things that have long since died. Much of the church's creativity is spent on trying to breathe life into old corpses. The church is right in its knowledge that it cannot do without its past traditions. The past, after all, contains all the promises of hope for the future which give momentum and direction to the world mission of the church. The traditions of promise, however, easily become a prison rather than a driving force of freedom. Changes are to be expected by the church to make way for the coming of God's kingdom. If the church lives toward the future of the Redeemer who has come and is on his way to the world now, the church will let itself become the instrument of change for the better. Standing still is the stratagem of regressive tendencies. But how can the church cope with change in a joyful way, rather than be doubled up by cramps of anxiety about the future? It must revive its eschatological consciousness, in short, live by the gospel which lifts its eyes to the hills of God's future. This means to live in anticipation of the power of God to transform the world. Keeping the picture of hope alive for a commonwealth of peace on earth and the brotherhood of mankind, the church will continue to issue its prophetic call for change. It will not glorify the status quo or any golden age in the past, for it will have a vivid vision of the great gap between the history of mankind to date and its promised future in the kingdom of God's freedom, love, and justice. The eschatological perspective opens the church to the future of the promises and calls it to prepare the world for what lies ahead. The gospel of the kingdom of God calls the church to the mission of hope to the nations and the politics of the kingdom in the world.

4. THE FUTURE OF THE CHRISTIAN MISSION

The missionary imperative of the church arises from the universal vision of its eschatological faith. No doubt the Western churches seem to have forfeited their right to mission by presuming upon advantages that colonial powers arrogated to themselves in non-Western lands. If that were all there were to it, missionaries could go home and forget the "great century" of missionary outreach as a bad dream of religious imperialism. But there is more to it than that. White men may repent of their evil, and should. But the universal mission to the nations comes from a message that does not belong to the church to do with as it pleases. The message of God's future belongs to world history; the church can betray or forget that message, but it cannot own it. Theology of mission faces a number of difficulties, but they in turn open up new opportunities.

1) It can be safely said that the theological capital that backed up the foreign missionary movement of Western Christianity is now depleted. The accounts have been closed down, not merely by theological developments but by basic changes in the world situation. At first it was thought that these changes on the world scene, e.g., the postcolonial phenomena of nationalism, industrialization, urbanization, socialization, secularization, etc., called mainly for new missionary strategy and tactics on the part of the churches. It is becoming clear that the changes needed are more fundamental and radical. It is no longer a question of merely finding new ways to carry on overseas missions conceived in the same old way. The crisis in world mission today is not due to poor techniques; rather, what lies at the root of the trouble is confusion about the message.

The outburst of missionary zeal that sought to save souls

from everlasting hell may linger on in isolated pockets of old-fashioned piety. The memory of what moved our nineteenth-century fathers usually draws a smile; rarely does it excite our imaginations. Yet, the missionary imperative remains inabrogable: to proclaim the gospel of the kingdom of God to the ends of the earth until the end of time. But what we are doing when we do just that in the contemporary world situation is not at all clear. What changes in the world would it bring? What differences to the individual can it make now and in the long run?

2) A theology of mission today cannot escape the issue of secularization. Is the gospel an agent of secularization now attacking the old foundations of all world religions, including Christianity as a religion? Is the gospel a partner or an enemy of secularization? Is secularization a product of the preaching of the gospel in the West? If so, can Asia and Africa accept this product apart from its Christian presuppositions? The divorce between the gospel and the secularizing process seems to be happening in the West itself, with the result that a liberal humanism is replacing Christianity as the spiritual foundation of a secularized society. But then we have to ask whether humanism can be indefinitely sustained apart from the Christian soil from which it has sprung. This soil has been sown with the seeds of the gospel, and one of the things that has come up is secularization as a historic process.

This question of the precise relation between the gospel and secularization is the thorniest one that the Christian mission faces today. Without an answer the church will act as if it were bound and gagged. For if secularization is thought to be the enemy of the gospel, then the Christian mission is tempted to ally itself with all other religions which feel equally threatened. We need only recall how the International Missionary Council, meeting in Jerusalem in 1928, suggested that in view of the rise of secularism and materialism, Christianity ought to form a common front with the other religions. If, on the other hand, secularization is a product of the gospel, then the process of secularization may indirectly lead the way in preparing for a new hearing of the gospel in cultures wholly dominated by non-Christian religions.

Our understanding of the gospel's relation to the world religions or to modern secularization will have a decisive effect on Christian mission. Let us illustrate. If the gospel is bound to what philosophers of religion call the religious *a priori,* then Christianity may seek to embody itself in forms of myth and cult that are native to a people. Indigenization will mean using elements of the existing religions through which to transmit the message of God's approaching kingdom. If, however, it is just such elements which are rendered obsolete by the inrushing forces of secularization, then all indigenization of that sort becomes inevitably anachronistic. To the extent that the Christian mission has then succeeded, to that extent it has failed.

Should the gospel stand second to secularization as an aggression against the religious myths and cults of mankind? The great theologians of the era that has just slipped behind us—Barth, Bultmann, Bonhoeffer, and Tillich—did not solve this problem. Yet all of them radicalized our understanding of the ambiguous connections between the gospel and religion, on the one side, and between the gospel and secularization, on the other side. The line that runs from Barth through Bultmann and Bonhoeffer tried to disengage the Christian message from its traditional tie-up with religion. Hendrik Kraemer wrote the theology of mission for this viewpoint in his book *The Christian Message in a Non-Christian World.* The attack of secularization on the world religions did not need to be bemoaned here, because the essence of the Christian message had been removed from the sphere of religion as a human phenomenon to the transcendent world of divine revelation. Bultmann's demythologizing of the New Testament and Bonhoeffer's nonreligious interpretation of biblical concepts had a similar result—loosening the traditional links between the Christian gospel and the religiousness of man. Paul Tillich, however, cannot be included in the same line of thought. Tillich believed there was a religious dimension that will survive the onslaughts of secularization. Thus, the Christian mission must advance dialectically on two fronts: first, with respect to the world religions; and second, with respect to the forces of technology and secularization. The gospel is to be defined neither as the essence of religion nor as the motive of secularization. Still less is it the declared enemy of both.

3) Theology of mission oscillates between exclusivist and inclusivist attitudes. Traditional exclusivism viewed Christianity as the true religion that is fighting to displace all the more or less false religions of the world. Christian superiority attitudes and religious arrogance have been nourished by the idea of Christianity as the one and only saving religion. Even the liberal revision of exclusivism which viewed Christianity as the absolute religion, as the crowning fulfillment of the history of religions, was nothing but another device to support the White Western syndrome of superiority. The Barthian position is to be applauded for undermining the foundations of Christian imperialism. Yet, this innovation did not go far enough; it gave birth to a new dogmatic exclusivism which could not help but safeguard a privileged position for the Christian synthesis in the West. It shared some of the cramps of traditional exclusivism by limiting the freedom of the gospel to create new syncretisms in non-Western situations.

4) Theology of mission must take up the problem of syncretism as the acid test of the relevance of its own thinking.[29] The lack of nerve to promote syncretization allowed inadequate aims to control missionary theology. Thus mission could easily become the tool of colonial expansionism and empire-building. The African who made the following statement was only slightly exaggerating: "When the missionary came, he had the Bible and we the land. Now we have the Bible, but he has our land."[30] Can anyone read Frantz Fanon's *The Wretched of the Earth* without radically questioning the past aims of missionary action? The aim of the Pietists to save as many souls as possible from burning hell as well as the

aim of Catholics to plant the church—*ecclesia plantanda*—both carried an overload of ideological thought keeping the colonizing powers in their seats of authority and privilege. These Pietists and these Catholics brought the gospel under the most ambiguous circumstances. They can hardly be matched for sheer courage and zeal, but their aims cannot be ours any longer. Missions were organs of ecclesiastical or denominational and of national or cultural propaganda. Martin Kähler of Halle was groping toward a true insight when he warned the churches and missionary societies of the difference between propaganda and mission. The propagandist, he said, "tries to make exact copies of himself."[31]

The problem of syncretism reveals the failures of the Western missionary movement. Burdened by legalism and dogmatism, the Western missions made the natives so shy of syncretism that they became the ghettos for the preservation of the alien syncretisms of the West. A German Lutheran and a Roman Catholic congregation existing side by side in an African village clearly exhibit how foreign the syncretisms and how false to impose them on others. The history of Western Christianity is, after all, the story of both the success and the failure of syncretism. In a series of steps Christianity became Hellenistic, Roman, Germanic, Nordic, Anglo-Saxon, and American. If the younger churches are free to operate on the model of the West, they too must become as imaginatively syncretic. That is a risk, but it is also the only hope for a true indigeneity. Perhaps they can even do a better job by learning from the failure of the West. For the West offers many examples of a false indigeneity, of an excessive identification with the given culture, to the point that the salt has lost its savor. Luther's protest was against an excessive "Romanizing" of Christianity; the Confessing Church protested against an excessive "Aryanizing" of Christianity. Perhaps in the future an African prophet will have to arise to protest the preaching of a Black Messiah to black people, when that preaching loses its power to take them out of their slavery. In any case, no white man will be in the position to be that prophet. Our Christ has been a white Jesus too long for black people to heed our sermons.

5) A theology of mission today can incorporate the problem of syncretism in a fresh way within the horizon of an eschatologically oriented theology of history. The totality of world history is the field of the church's mission. Any flaw in eschatology will work itself out in the mission of the church to the nations. Churches that become turned in upon themselves or that seek to make carbon copies of themselves are acting from a false eschatology. The missionary myopia of the Reformers and their Orthodox successors can be traced to eschatology. If the Great Commission was already fulfilled in the time of the apostles, as they said, we no longer have to go to the whole world. The heathen today will be justly punished for their fathers' refusal to accept the gospel. Eschatology concerns only the bundle of things that will pile up at the end of history.

When Pietism revitalized missionary thinking, it did so from the perspective of the kingdom of God. That was a gain. But the kingdom of God in Pietism suffered from severe limitations. For one thing, its eschatological hope was so otherworldly that the coming of God's kingdom was detached from the actual events of world history. For another, it was oriented almost exclusively to the individual and the salvaging of his soul for life in another world. In short, its supernaturalistic otherworldliness and its individualistic soteriology stunted the hope for the *coming* of God's kingdom to the *world*.

6) The gospel of the kingdom of God is not news from another world about another world. It is a gospel born from the history of God in this world for the sake of this world's future in the kingdom of God. Missionary theology must always be formulated in light of the promise and hope that broke through the history that runs forward from the exodus of Israel to the resurrection of Jesus. History is exodus into the future of life that arrived in the person and destiny of Jesus of Nazareth. The only

future for the Christian mission is to bring the future of Christ
to bear on the destiny of mankind. The future of Christ can be
preached as hope for mankind because the resurrection is a prolepsis of a new world in which the deadliness of death has been relegated to the past. The gospel of the kingdom of God is the announcement of the future of life, *shalom,* and righteousness for
man and his world. The symbol of the kingdom of God includes
not only personal but also social and political dimensions of hope
for fulfillment beyond ambiguity and negativity, as we shall try
to show in our next chapter. The gospel speaks to the whole man
and the whole of his culture. The gospel does not seek to insert
itself into the religious slot in other cultures, leaving everything
else as it is. In being preached from Jerusalem to the ends of the
earth, the gospel is a power to make new history by transforming
all existing things. The revolutionary force in the gospel is released into history from the future of God, as a process to make
all things new.

7) The gospel of the kingdom represents a total claim by
preaching the lordship of Christ in relation to the totality of life,
individually and socially. Therefore, it has been a true missionary
instinct when education and medicine have been accompaniments
of mission. But these tasks are provisional and temporary. The
church stands in for the political community as its substitute when
it cares for people through schools and hospitals. When the political community matures and becomes strong enough to accept
responsibility for these needs, the church should cheerfully relin-
quish its hold on these functions and direct its energies elsewhere.
The church should not wait until it is squeezed out of these functions by the state, but in every way goad the state to assume its
responsibilities as well and as quickly as possible. That is what
it means for the church to be the vanguard of the kingdom in the
social sphere.

8) Even in a society that reaches our highest social and
political expectations (such a society has never existed), the church

has the indispensable task of witnessing to the ultimate goal and meaning of life, thus bestowing on individuals a sense of personal worth that can never be exhausted by the individual's social, economic, or political functions. In the presence of the eternal future of God, the significance of the present moment of the individual is heightened beyond its pragmatic value to the social and political community. In Harnack's famous phrase, "the infinite value of the individual soul" is something that entered deeply into human consciousness through the message of Jesus the Messiah. The eternal future of the individual may not be sacrificed to social well-being in the present. That would be to dwarf the imagination that lives from the power of the absolute future in the life of God.

FIVE

The Politics of
Hope - Society

1. TOWARD A THEOLOGY OF REVOLUTION

No word is used more frequently to describe the present world situation than the word "revolution." The world as a whole and all its parts are being confronted by the demands of revolutionary change. Already in 1942 Paul Tillich spoke of the revolutionary nature of the changes we face as the "storms of our times"[1] and put the question whether the church and its theology would be able to cope with the revolutionary transformation of the world and of human existence. The pressures on theology to take up the theme of revolution have been mounting. In 1966 a world study conference at Geneva took up the theme "Christians in the Technical and Social Revolutions of Our Time." The theological contributions were weak, almost nonexistent.[2] This is not surprising when we consider that for centuries theologians have been producing systems in which the virtues of harmony, order, and stability have been stressed. Delegates to the conference from the

Third World (Africa, Asia, and South America) were hoping to hear from theologians a "theology of revolution" which could equip them for the revolutionary struggles in their own lands. Harvey Cox has seen the problem which not only these Christians but all Christians face: "We are trying to live in a period of revolution without a theology of revolution. The development of such a theology should be the first item on the theological agenda today."[3]

But why would we need a *theology* of revolution? Is not that a terrifying mixing of categories or confusing of horizons? We define a theology of revolution as the politics of eschatological hope in society. In order to practice Christian hope for the world, we must reflect on whether or how God may be active in revolutionary situations. There is a very practical reason why we as Christians need a theology of revolution. Without it we will be at a total loss about what to do for the rest of the century. Hannah Arendt in her book *On Revolution* has predicted that even though mankind has the good sense to set aside war as an international political instrument, revolutions will continue into the foreseeable future to make this a century of revolutions. Then she says that "in the contest which divides the world today and in which so much is at stake, those will probably win who understand revolution."[4] Christians must understand revolution, not to win a political contest as such but because they cannot escape responsibility for the outcome. The stakes are high—the future of man, the scale of justice, the quality of freedom, the shape of society. The ultimate concern of the Christian is not one which lies outside these secular interests but one which seeks a formative expression through them. The religious relationship between man and God does not run alongside of the relationship of both to the world. The commandment to love God has no substance at all apart from love to the neighbor.[5]

There are other reasons why the church must develop a theology of revolution. The church is to a large extent responsible for the revolutionary consciousness that is emerging around the world. A common reaction in the West is to blame Communism for spreading the revolutionary virus. That is to give it far too much credit. To be sure, many Christians who are ignorant of history and misunderstand the gospel rally around counterrevolutionary crusades, leaving it to Communists to be apostles of change and missionaries of a revolutionary movement. But the seeds of revolutionary dreams and hopes were scattered far and wide by the preaching of a gospel whose very essence is revolution. In the chapter "The Revolutionary West," in his book *Christianity in World History*, A. T. van Leeuwen ascribes the revolutionary impulse in the West to the revolutionizing impact of the gospel of the coming kingdom of God.[6] Indirectly the church has sponsored the revolutionary process by preaching a message which sets things in motion by stirring up the imagination, arousing new expectations, and stimulating a crusading zeal to translate hopes, whose realization some would postpone for heaven above, already into the social structures of this world. The simple fact of preaching the gospel is like putting sticks of dynamite into the social structure. The church is responsible for having planted many charges of dynamite into beloved structures that it at the time had no desire to explode, since its own privilege were beholden to them.

A theology of revolution is made all the more urgent by the fact that the Christian churches must repent of the inglorious role they have played in most modern revolutionary situations. While the gospel they preached pointed the way of hope for the future, the institutions they built impeded its coming. The official churches —as well as church officials—have been guilty of betraying the promises of the gospel for the sake of securing alliances with the classes tenured with privileges of power, property, and position. Here lies the major reason for the anti-Christian character of modern revolutionary movements. The eschatological message of Christianity has been turned against the church. The modern conflict between Western Christianity and Marxism may be a case of two heresies fighting each other. The driving force in Marxism is its secularized version of the eschatological dynamic of the Bible. When the church loses this dynamic, it becomes a conservative institution, forcing the present into the mold of the past, favoring those in the present who inherit the benefits of the past's unjust structures. A theology of revolution will call the church to repentance, not in the individualistic terms it has piously cherished for its faithful but in socially concrete terms. The only way into the kingdom of God is through a repentance that involves the whole man. Today we perhaps see more clearly than our forebears that the "whole man" is never an isolated individual *coram deo*. He exists in solidarity with the society of which he is a part. Repentance in face of the approaching kingdom of God means that the church will not only not stand in the way of its coming but will involve itself at the front lines of changing things for the sake of a new and better order. The attempt to seek every possible approximation of its eschatological hopes already in this life, in this world, will inevitably create revolutionary situations.

A theology of revolution thus seeks to express the social and political ethic of a church whose faith has been renewed by the rediscovery of the genuinely revolutionary theology of hope in the Bible. The spirit of revolution is enflamed by an eschatological message that reacts upon world history. For the very essence of the spirit of revolution is not the bloody violence, which is often its tragic accompaniment, but zeal for new things, eagerness to usher in a *novus ordo saeculorum*. There are unbloody revolutions. Bloody violence is usually the result of a tragic collision between the new and the old, whenever the gap between the new and the old orders has grown so wide that it cannot be bridged by creative transitions. Partisans of the old order have neglected to build bridges to the future, and thus unwittingly guarantee that the new order will be constructed without them. This is tragic, because the new order becomes empty and fanatic without the humanizing values which have sustained themselves in the tradition. A theology of revolution is needed to prepare the church to play a creative and healing role in the tragic tension between the old and the new, between revolution and reaction, novelty and tradition. If the institutional church continues to identify its interests with the forces of reaction and counterrevolution, it will be guaranteeing its exclusion from the new order of the world. And the gates of hell will have prevailed against the form of the church we now know. The ax will fall at the roots, and a new shoot will have to arise on the other side of catastrophe. This age of revolution will be a test whether the church belongs to the past that cannot survive the onslaught of the new or whether it will bring the freshest word of newness and stir up an eagerness in people to seek a new order of things in every postrevolutionary situation. Is the church a demonstration of that newness that never grows old with time? If so, then it is because its life-creating message is grounded in that absolute future which has broken into history already in Jesus Christ and the Word of the Gospel that announces the coming of his kingdom to the nations. A theology of revolution cannot be an appendix to theology merely to bring it up to date. Such a theology must be composed of the elements for reflection that broke into human consciousness through the appearance of the ultimate future of man and his world in Jesus Christ.

2. A CRITIQUE OF THE TWO-KINGDOM DOCTRINE

A theology of revolution begins with the extreme liability of running counter to the political ethic of the church that has dominated its thinking during the entire Constantinian era. It carries the burden of having the main weight of the church's tradition against it. This tradition was formulated for Western Christianity by Augustine, and at the time of the Reformation, Luther and Calvin rendered it in their own way. All of them, however, are fundamentally conservative and antirevolutionary. When Augustine identified the hierarchy of the church with the kingdom of God in history,[7] and placed the destinies of the City of God and the City of Earth outside each other, he laid the foundation for both a church-centeredness and a dualism that cuts the veins that run from the kingdom of God through the body of this world. This led to a conservative ecclesiocentric interpretation of history. Luther's two-kingdom doctrine was to a great extent modeled after Augustine's two-city doctrine. As Heinrich Bornkamm states: "Here is the root and soil of Luther's two kingdom doctrine."[8] Our interest here is not to give an account of the doctrines of either Augustine or Luther, nor to mention any subtleties of difference between them. An enormous effort has been made, especially by Lutheran scholars, to free Luther's doctrine of any liabilities it might have incurred through the history of Lutheranism. A recovery of Luther's two-kingdom doctrine is hailed as sufficient to provide the church today with its political ethic. One defender of this viewpoint has written, "There is nothing so sick about Lutheran ethics that a strong dose of Luther cannot cure it."[9] It would be quite delightful if that were the case. May the rescue operation continue in the name of Luther research! However, any proper prescription depends on the nature and extent of the illness. The problem is that Luther's two-kingdom doctrine itself, even when the best construction is placed upon it, as, for example, by Heinrich Bornkamm or Ulrich Asendorf,[10] leads to a conservative political ethic in which the question of revolution is invariably answered in the negative. I see no way to elude the judgment of Paul Tillich that Luther's political ethic was nonrevolutionary both theoretically and practically.[11] It is, of course, absurd to draw a straight line from that to Hitler and the sins of modern Luthernism. But there may still be a crooked line—an interesting subject which we will gladly leave for the Luther scholars to debate.

The problem is not that a Lutheran may not, if he has the will to do so, make room for most any political or social ideal within the framework of the two-kingdom doctrine. For although

Luther could easily justify his actions in the Peasants' Revolt by his political ethic, one could conceivably reach an opposite conclusion within the same ethic. After all, allowance was made by both Luther and the Augsburg Confession for something we today would call "civil disobedience."[12] This could take the form of resisting temporal authorities, of breaking any human law in violation of the law of God, or of refusing to bear arms in a manifestly unjust war. However, the churchman who has had the 20/20 vision to tell a just war from an unjust one has been a rare bird indeed. Yet, the ethical principle on which one may decline to serve one's government in waging an unjust war exists within the two-kingdom doctrine, although that principle has never been invoked by a Lutheran church and rarely by any of its members.

The exceptional clause in the two-kingdom ethic which might justify an *ad hoc* act of defiance of established authorities, even when it reaches the stage of outright revolt, does not and can not motivate a revolutionary transformation of the established order of things—because the eschatological dynamic is missing. The aim of a rebellion is to restore what has been lost; the aim of revolution is to create something new. The vision of the radically new is what links revolutionary action with eschatological hope. The problem with the two-kingdom doctrine is that the revolutionary dynamic discharged by the kingdom on the right hand did not set off any explosions in the kingdom on the left hand. There is manifestly a defective eschatology at work here. The dynamics of the coming kingdom of God have had profound effects upon the inner life of faith, reaching unequaled depths in the spirituality of a Kierkegaard. But it is the dynamics of quite another kingdom at work in the realm of social and political life. This means that the gospel may stir up a revolutionary storm only within the individual, never within society. The spiritual life of the Lutheran Christian is in a state of constant crisis; there the whole impact of the coming kingdom of God is experienced in judgment and forgiveness. The political and social characteristics of the biblical symbol of the kingdom of God have been suppressed in favor of the religious experience of the individual person.[13]

The positive assets of the two-kingdom doctrine need not be lost in a reformulation of an eschatological ethic that points to the transformation of the world. The elements of truth in the two-kingdom doctrine are many, but here we point out only what is important for a revolutionary ethic. In distinguishing between two kingdoms, both of which are God's, it was possible for Lutherans to develop a theology of power which did not shrink from seeing it as the "strange work" of God's love. This is a revolutionary idea itself, for many an ethic of love has withered in the face of the show of power. How can power and love be united with each other? The two-kingdom ethic was an attempt to say that Christians are not to retreat from power situations in the secular realm, because that realm is God's and he is the source of all power. Christians may thus "occupy civil offices or serve as princes and judges, render decisions and pass sentence according to imperial and other existing laws, punish evil doers with the sword, engage in just wars, serve as soldiers, buy and sell, take required oaths, possess property, be married, etc."[14] The Lutheran doctrine went on to condemn the position held by those sectarians who so zoomed off into the future of God's eschatological *shalom* that they withdrew from social and political responsibility. On the other hand, Lutheran doctrine taught Christians merely to *uphold* the secular orders, not to *change* them. The purpose of power is to serve as a dike against sin, to forestall chaos, to preserve law and order. The given situation as we know it must be defended against revolutionary change and radical progress. The two-kingdom doctrine has invariably engendered a conservative political ethic because the eschatological dynamic of the gospel is not released into the power situations which decide for or against the inner-historical transformation of society. Its theology of power, essential also in a revolutionary ethic, is made to serve the interests of the status quo. Its theology of power has been wedded to a static conception of the world. Hence, it has never been difficult to justify the use of power by a police force or a national army, for these use power to keep things as they are. Since revolutionary power always changes things and frequently threatens chaos and anarchy, one has assumed that God's will is on the side of change-lessness. To obey God's providential will is to resign oneself to the powers that be and to operate within the given system. This is a positivistic doctrine of God's providence.

The two-kingdom doctrine cannot support a revolutionary ethic as long as the realm of creation does not share the same eschatological future as the realm of redemption. Tillich, who broke with a static form of the two-kingdom doctrine in becoming a religious socialist, put it this way: "Its most obvious shortcoming is the fact that it contrasts the salvation of the individual with the transformation of the historical group and the universe, thus sepa-rating the one from the other."[15] The church is then understood as the sphere in which individuals experience salvation and the outside world as somehow excluded from the future which Christ has pioneered. The kingdom of God toward which the church is pressing and for whose coming it prays in the Lord's Prayer is the goal also of the nations and kingdoms of this earth.[16] The essential eschatological basis of the social and political dimensions of the church's message to the world is missing in the two-king-dom doctrine. The doctrines of creation and redemption are in-adequately linked to the eschatological goal of both the church and the world in the future of God's coming kingdom. One could say that while there is an eschatology of redemption in this doctrine, there is no eschatology of creation. This lack of an eschatological alignment of the doctrine of creation made it possible later to declare the orders of creation completely autonomous and beyond the church's concern. The gap between the church's sphere of responsibility, namely, preaching the Word and administering the sacraments, and the secular spheres in which people live out their daily lives, widened to the point where its message, in itself revolutionary, became unintelligible to the masses of people. It became detached from the situations charged with revolutionary unrest. When modern revolutions exploded on the face of the earth, the church was unprepared to understand and too ill equipped to participate in the struggles waged by peasants, by the proletariat, and by the desperately poor and miserable. The very ones in whose midst the signs of the messianic kingdom are to erupt are those from whom the church has managed to estrange itself, for the Messiah comes, we are told, when "the blind see, the lame walk, lepers are cleansed, the deaf hear, the dead are raised up, and the poor are hearing good news."[17] If the church's eschatological message creates a pathway of hope for the poor, the bearer of that message, the church, will have to take responsibility for seeking some earthly cash value for that hope in concrete social and economic terms. Today almost everywhere this calls for nothing less than a revolutionary transformation of society from the top down. The two-kingdom ethic has sponsored charity institutions. In many cases, however, these have inadvertently helped to prolong the life of unjust social structures by relieving the pain of their most visible casualties. The zeal for revolution flags when the pain is soothed.[18] A new revolutionary praxis of the church will alone be able to answer the charge that religion itself serves as a pain-killer passed out in sufficient doses to numb the nerve of potential revolutionaries.

The two-kingdom doctrine stresses the actual difference between God's rule of power (*regnum potentiae*) in the world and his rule of grace (*regnum gratiae*) through the gospel. The Achilles' heel of this doctrine is that it lingers with this contrast, rather than pressing for earthly signs which foreshadow its ultimate resolution in the common future of the church and the world in God's rule of glory (*regnum gloriae*). The dynamic eschatology of the gospel invades this world, holding up social and political symbols of its future, and not only solutions to the existential problems of the inner life. The doctrine of the two kingdoms has led to a static conception of the church and the world standing alongside each other, each one jealously guarding its own turf, refusing to be encroached upon by the other. At its best this doctrine has worked to police the borders between the church and the world, and even to encourage harmony, cooperation, mutual good will, and "functional interaction."[19] The present advocates of the two-kingdom doctrine are attempting to overcome the sort of dualism which has led to tragic historical consequences. They say that the two kingdoms are not at all divided; they are united in the person of the Christian individual who is moved by a "faith active in love" to serve his neighbors in the secular arena. The dynamic of life in the secular realm is the forgiveness of sins. One can joyfully take up one's secular tasks without having to find one's justification in them. The kingdom on the left hand of God is the realm in which the phenomena of law and justice, reason and power, threats and punishments, hold sway. The kingdom on the right hand is the realm of God's saving work in Christ, realized on earth through the church's preaching of the gospel and administration of the sacraments. In this realm the phenomena of faith and love, joy and peace, hope and freedom, prevail. It may be useful to make such distinctions, but if they are separated, or united only in the *person* of the individual Christian, the results are catastrophic. It means, in short, that the eschatological dynamics of the gospel, the social and political features of the onrushing kingdom of God, are diverted from their aim to transform this world. When they are released into the world, they set in motion waves of revolutionary expectations that threaten structures of injustice and inequality. What a travesty if the justice of the kingdom of God, experienced now as the gift of forgiveness on account of Christ, should not inspire new and greater visions of justice for the world. The distinction between "rich and poor," which Hannah Arendt says had always been assumed to be a natural one,[20] built into the eternal structure of things, was first broken down by those whose imaginations were fired by an eschatological vision of freedom from want and plenty for all. It is only by anticipating a new world that we gain freedom from bondage to the presumably immutable order of things. "The poor you will always have with you"—an occasional utterance of Jesus—is turned into a universal law of nature by Christian realists who have lost their eschatology.

The stress on the *two* kingdoms has cautioned against two possible dangers, that of a "Christianization of society" by ecclesiastical heteronomy, remaking the world into the image of the church, or of a "secularization of the church," remaking the church into the image of the world. Both of these dangers can be avoided, without remaining impaled on the dualism of the two kingdoms, only by reactivating the kingdom-of-God eschatology of the Bible, emphasizing not a spatial duality of spheres but the temporal difference between the "already now" and the "not yet," that is, the present and the future aspects of the power of God's rule.

3.   CHRISTIAN PROPHETS OF REVOLUTION

The Marxist charge that religion is a "mystical opiate" to quench revolutionary impulses does not fit all the facts. There is a revolutionary strain in the religious traditions of both Judaism and Christianity, from which the prophetic elements in Marxism are derived. There have been undercurrents of revolution in the Christian tradition, breaking up the logjams of history by their dynamic thrust toward the future. The Christian prophets of revolution, imbued by visions of the end of history, have been dismissed by the conservative tradition as blurry-eyed enthusiasts, crazy chiliasts. Luther lumped them all together as *"Schwärmer."* This will no longer do. A revolutionary ethic will recover the passion for the future which possessed the enthusiasts, finding in their eschatology an urgent corrective of the conservative tradition.

The French Marxist philosopher Roger Garaudy sees that the history of the church is "criss-crossed by this internal dialectic, this inherent opposition between the Constantinian tradition . . . and the apocalyptic tradition."[21] As the apocalyptic tradition gains ground over the Constantinian, Christianity can no longer be attacked as opium of the ruling classes. Again it will be the leaven it originally was to raise marvelous expectations for the future of man. As a religious socialist, Tillich upgraded the Christian revolutionary tradition and drew many of his categories from the sectarian radicals for his own theory of revolution. Heinz-Dietrich Wendland has written that Paul Tillich was the first and almost the only important theologian who dealt with the question of "the connection between the revolutionary element in the Christian message and revolution in history."[22] Tillich was especially sympathetic with Joachim of Fiore's revolutionary theology of history. He saw it as a precursor of the line that ran from the radical Franciscans through the left-wing reformers to the proletarian utopians of today. "In all these movements the future is the decisive mode of time."[23] The golden age does not lie in the past. Something really new is expected from the future which goes beyond the past or present forms of the church and its social milieu. What makes Joachim's theology of history revolutionary is the idea that the past can be criticized and the present transformed under the impact of the future.[24] Joachim called this imminent future the third stage or period, the age of the Spirit. There is no classical period of church history to which every new present must conform by repristinating old forms. The past and the present are preparations for something new in the future. This is in line with Jesus' saying that his followers would do even greater works than he had done.[25] Joachim's doctrine of the three overlapping stages which mark out periods in history reflecting the threefold nature of God, and his artificial speculations about dates and generations, are not what makes this theology of history revolutionary. As with all speculative predictions, history can prove them wrong. Joachim's computation that the age of the Holy Spirit must begin A.D. 1260 sounds funny to us. The revolutionary element in his thinking is not thereby invalidated. The fact remains that he expected from the future new patterns, new forms, new creations, which would revolutionize the church and society. This future is filled with the new things the Spirit alone can create. The existing institutions of the church and society are prototypes that point the way to future fulfillment. Thus, there is continuity between the old and the new, between the first two stages and the third. And there is progress. But for Joachim this continuity and this progress pass through death on the way to rebirth and future fulfillment.

Eschatological prophets are not always revolutionary. Some have had visions of the future and have dropped out of society. But others have expected the speedy coming of a new age and have hastened to prepare its way. The promise of a really new future can trigger off revolutionary impulses in the present. This was the case with Thomas Münzer.[26] He wanted more than a reformation of the church; he wanted a revolution of society. A church that is interested only in its self-reformation must have tamed the eschatological impulses of the Word of God that are aimed also at society. Münzer was a "theologian of revolution," as the title of Ernst Bloch's book of 1921 puts it, who despaired of reforming the old church structures. Nothing less than a new form of the church is needed. He called on his followers to "stick out their necks" in building a new church and a new society. Ernst Benz states that "through Münzer, Joachimitism enters its revolutionary phase in Germany."[27] Münzer knew Joachim's writings and tried to apply his revolutionary ideas. We cannot recount here the tragic story of Münzer, whose revolution was aborted by the power of the princes and ended with his execution in 1525.

Münzer's ideas lived on to influence others. He makes one ponder the question, valid in our time also, whether in a given situation we should work for gradual improvement of existing institutions, however archaic or corrupt, or discard them by revolutionary action, even at the risk of our necks. A look at the pro-revolutionary tradition in the church might reinforce our doubts that the policy of gradualism or accelerated evolutionary change is always preferable or even possible. Münzer's dream of a new society saw no place for blood aristocracy, status privileges, class rankings, and the exploitation of the weak by the strong. These were revolutionary ideas, fired by his mystical experiences, and activated by his confidence in the coming kingdom. The connection between eschatology and revolution becomes unmistakable in the structure of Münzer's thought. It is not an existentially necessary connection, for eschatology has also been invoked to favor escapist attitudes toward the world, also in primitive Christianity. Yet, the connection is there and has been documented by many social historians.[28]

4. DYNAMIC PRINCIPLES OF THE KINGDOM

The prime requisite for a theology of revolution is to shift from the statics of traditional ontology to the dynamics of eschatology. The traditional ontology which the church fathers took over from Hellenistic philosophy became hostile to the dynamic picture of reality as history opening toward the future. What would be involved for a theology of revolution in a shift back to an eschatological way of thinking in which the future holds the primacy?

The creation and the fall will be viewed in light of the God of exodus and the eschaton. Not vice versa. God is not the creator of an eternal order which is lamentably set in motion by man's fall into sin. He is not the supreme being presiding over a world whose end is but a restoration of the beginning. He is the God of history whose end is something new. The movement from exodus to the eschaton is not to regain a paradise lost, to return to the "good old days." The world is not a closed cosmos within which things recur cyclically; it is a project which is now under way toward a future goal. To reach that goal the world must be changed, transformed by the power of God's creative future. History moves forward to the kingdom of God. On the way there are novelties, surprises, new starts, dead ends, tragedies, and glimmerings of fulfillment.

The way by which God's future becomes creative of new history is through death and resurrection. A Christian theology of revolution is messianic. The road from exodus to the eschaton leads through the passion, death, and burial of Jesus Christ. Fulfillment in a new creation happens on the other side of suffering and sacrifice. Victory can come through defeat. A theology of revolution must have as its primary paradigm the death and resurrection of Jesus Christ. The chief cornerstone of the new construction is the stone which the builders rejected. Christian participation in revolution is the way of the cross. A passionate struggle for justice brings with it a cross. Christians must believe that what counts in a revolution which has the future on its side is not a democratic majority. The axial point of the shifting of aeons was a minority of one condemned by the Roman government as a zealot, a political insurrectionist. The salvation event was at the same time a political event. The bearers of the future development of history are those in whom there is an intense consciousness of what is going on in history, the vanguard. The Bible calls them the remnant. In a pluralistic world in which Christianity is likely to become a minority religion in the future it is well to remember that the future has never been voted into existence by the masses of people.

Jesus is the eschatological word-event in world history because in him the final word from the future of God has been spoken back into history. This word creates a future for us and exercises a hope for the future of the world. It is not a passive, idle hope. It seeks a speedy and full realization of that for which it hopes.

Eschatological hope that is created by the absolute future in Jesus makes Christian life cruciform. This marks the difference between the Christian revolutionary and any other. For the Christian, reality itself is cruciform, as Rosenstock-Huessy says.[29] As the cross has four bars, there are four fronts on which to fight: the past and the future, the individual and the social. The Christian revolutionary cannot sacrifice everything for the future as if the past is meaningless and the present a mere stepping-stone to something that always lies ahead. This makes of the future a Moloch on whose altar we sacrifice both our brothers and the gifts of history. The Christian will not lose the past, because it also belongs to the future summed up in Christ. By the same token, he will not sacrifice the future to the past. He is free both from the terrors of the future and from the tyranny of the past. And that is what makes him loose and fit for revolutionary action. He is exonerated from the illusion that without him and his group the world would go to hell.

Reality that stretches backward and forward also comprises the individual and the social. The Christian revolutionary will not be swept along by movements which sacrifice the elements of subjectivity and transcendence for the sake of a collectivistic society of "one-dimensional men."[30] Nor will he be bewitched by an aristocratic ideal of personality which indulges itself at the expense of the common good. The Christian revolutionary who fights on all "four fronts" is more of a revolutionary than the one for whom reality does not appear in light of the cross.

The Christian revolutionary is pulled forward by the vision of the coming kingdom of God. He is not pushed headlong into the future by the trends of the past. A computer can predict the future by the current trends. The Christian believes that a qualitatively different future can be created, actually reversing the trends of the times. The Christian is free to seek a victory over trends and well-established structures. The clues and hints he has to go by are the ones suggested by the proleptic revelation of the kingdom of God in Jesus. Here he has a promise of the future for whose coming he is invited to act. His actions are guided by goals. The eschatological end radically justifies the ethical means. Nothing else can. This means that he is not guided by universal laws of nature, unalterable principles inscribed into the granitelike structure of things—the same yesterday, today, and forevermore. The natural-law theory which Christian theology inherited from the Greek and Roman philosophers is ill-suited to an eschatological ethos.[31] The difference is that an ethic derived from eschatology is geared to history as a realm of intentions, free decisions, new situations, and unique events. The idea of natural law was created in terms of a metaphysical picture of the world-as-nature, rather than an eschatological picture of the world-as-history.

The dynamics of the kingdom of God *in* history must not be swallowed up in the statics of the symbol of eternal life *beyond* history. The kingdom of God is often preached as an anchor of hope for the individual soul in an eternal realm outside of history. It is more than this. It is the power of the future manifesting itself in political and social terms, in the struggle for peace with justice, for solidarity with personal freedom. The kingdom of God struggles in history to break the tyranny of the strong over the weak, to liberate men from authoritarian systems of power, and to rescue individuals from depersonalizing mechanisms. The kingdom of God scores a victory when community is built between nations and when the unity of mankind is advanced, when higher unities are built without war and when peace on earth makes mutual fulfillment of individuals and nations possible. A two-kingdom ethic which says that these are merely secular, and not soteriological, concerns has made the fatal mistake of divorcing salvation history from world history. The penultimates of history must not be detached from the ultimate which defines their place. The churches are to represent the full scope of the kingdom of God in history, not merely those aspects of it which refer to the inner-personal life.

The function of the church in the political realm is to release new impulses which might raise the level of expectations, to inject hope into society, giving birth to vision and courage to transform existing institutions. Its witness will make clear that all present forms of social life are ambiguous and at very best only partial approximations of the kingdom of God. A prophetic church criticizes the present in light of the promised future of the kingdom. Its eschatological vision is the basis of its realism. The church can thus reject the temptation to absolutize any political or social form of life. It will relativize all historical realizations in light of the final goal of history—the absolute future. It cannot help but stir up discontent in society by goading men on to more perfect forms of life. It will not suffer the illusion, meanwhile, of secular utopianism that the perfection of life can be attained apart from the intervention of God.

The way of the kingdom of God in history is not a progressive development in a straight line or a smooth rhythm. Judgment and chaos may become the needle's eye through which we must pass before renewal and social progress are possible. The antirevolutionary bias of the churches has assumed that the kingdom of God suffers a defeat in every revolution. The kingdom of God is thought to be on the side of tradition, immobility, and in general the values of the older generations. It would now be an equally great mistake for radical Christians to add their blessing to every new revolution. The kingdom of God may be said to triumph when a revolution succeeds in creating new conditions of equality, justice, and freedom without sacrificing the richness of past expressions of creativity. There are humane and rational traditions which are threatened by every revolutionary upheaval. When a conflict between the old and new can be resolved in a higher synthesis, the pains of social growth are lessened and catastrophes avoided. Who wins? The kingdom of God wins—for man! That is the way of the kingdom of God in history, and that is how a political ethic may be informed by a reinstatement of the eschatological pole in Christian theology.

Modern revolutionary ideology tends to become conservative in the postrevolutionary situation. The dynamics born by the spirit of revolution are played out in the defense of the new achieve-ments and new institutions. Belief in the coming of God's king-dom relativizes the revolution and criticizes its self-absolutizing tendencies. The Christian always looks forward in hope for the kingdom that is still to come, and by exercising this hope he is critical of everything that already is. Revolutionaries who win are tempted to stabilize the new status quo and to set up a "reign of terror" against those who would continue the revolutionary spirit of criticism. Hannah Arendt states: "The failure of post-revolution-ary thought to remember the revolutionary spirit and to under-stand it conceptually was preceded by the failure of the revolution to provide it with a lasting institution."[32] None of the major modern revolutions has found a device to keep the revolutionary spirit alive. "The spirit of revolution . . . has failed to find its appropriate institution."[33] Hannah Arendt turns to the poets as those who alone can compensate for this failure, because they watch over the storehouse of memory and "make the words we live by."[34] All due credit to the poets. But what about the proph-ets? And the people of the Messiah? Christians who are con-scious of their eschatological calling will pursue a politics of hope to keep the fires of criticism hot until the messianic kingdom comes in final judgment and in all its glory. They watch over that storehouse of memory charged with the promises of God that, standing out in front of all present achievements, rekindle the hopes to have them come true. The expectation of the future of God's kingdom is the only lasting institution Christians know of to keep the revolutionary spirit young when the warriors become old. This spirit of revolution cannot be institutionalized.

5. THE CHURCH AND THE REVOLUTION TODAY

The churches today are groping toward a creative role in the revolutions of our time. The world is volcanic and the lava of revolution is being thrown out upon the face of the earth in judgment. The churches can join the forces of inertia and reaction, or they can cooperate with those who hope and act for a better future for man on earth. The revolutionary outbursts of today challenge the churches to search the deep things of their eschatological faith, better to take hold of history, to see without illusions, to love without fear. What will the churches say and what will they do in a revolutionary age? The gap is widening between the rich and the poor countries. There is no existing structure of world economic order and justice to reverse the trend. Revolution arises when the poor become hopeless in their poverty, and the rich cling to systems which keep them on top. Richard Shaull alerts us to the danger of a "Pax Russo-Americana"[35] which would place the rich nations on one side against the underdeveloped countries. No longer is the major conflict in the world the ideological one between East and West. It is the economic abyss that divides North and South. A revolutionary change in international economy is demanded. Van Leeuwen offers the slogan "economic democracy for the world"[36] as a new concept fully consistent with the church's vision of the kingdom of God. Western Christianity has helped to create in poor people a burning desire for personal dignity and a higher standard of material welfare. What will be done now when it becomes clear that these desires can be met only by overthrowing existing structures? Western affluence was made possible by such things as democracy, science, technology, a work-ethic, and the secularization of nature—all of them by-products of Christian influence. Other nations need and want these things. But a great gulf seems to be fixed between Dives, the rich man, and Lazarus.

The rich nations also happen to be the white nations, and in American society the poor happen to be black. The racial element is part of the revolutionary potential in the world. White liberals like to say they are color-blind, but the slogan "Black Power" is freeing them of their illusion. The "secular city," which Harvey

Cox presents as the modern translation of the long-awaited kingdom of God, has not yet arrived. Cox says that a theology of
revolution must make a place for catastrophe.[37] This may cause
us "to change, to repent, to revolt."[38] Many of Cox's critics missed
the apocalyptic note of catastrophe in their first reading of *The
Secular City*. So did I. But it is there, and it has since taken the
form of burning down the "secular city." A city cannot be a paradise for the white man as long as it is a hell for the black person.
Will the Christian vision of the New Jerusalem be brought down
from the heights of apocalypse into history in time to avert the
catastrophe that is bound to occur if our existing systems of racial
injustice are permitted to continue? The leaders of Black Power
have learned the language of revolution. Long ago they must have
had the feelings. Christians ought to understand that revolutionary
feelings are not willed. They happen wherever human misery is
no longer bearable. Carl Oglesby writes that the initial revolutionary motive is not to construct a paradise but to destroy an in-
ferno.[39] The Christian should know the difference. The one who
lives in the infernal conditions of poverty and injustice cannot be
exhorted to have respect for law and order. "The rebel is someone
for whom injustice and society are only different words for the
same thing."[40] The revolutionary, Oglesby says, is the revolted
one, the one who is being reduced to his revulsion,[41] who dares
to be irresponsible because he alone has no stakes. He is brought
to the "edge of violence" . . . "totally possessed by his predicament" . . . "fused with his futurelessness" . . . "turned
into venom" . . . "a dead-earnest soldier who has accepted
death."[42] This anatomy of the revolutionary psyche is not given
to exacerbate the situation. It will seem extremist only to those
who hope that problems will be solved without changing anything.
    There are those who today speak in terms of "total revolu-
tion." What is implied is that the major institutions of society are
in cahoots to keep the total system as it is. Capital and labor, big
government and the military, provide checks and balances in rela-

tion to one another, but together they take pitiably meager measures to make room for those outside the system. The established order can further perpetuate itself by controlling technology and the mass media. Mass conformity in the West can become as totalitarian as the Communism it has so much feared in the East. The mainstream of the Western way of life is something into which many people do not wish to be integrated, and some of those already in it are looking for ways to "drop out." Writing about the New Left and young radicals, Richard Shaull says: "Participation in movements for social change leads many young people to take a revolutionary position *vis-à-vis* the whole established order."[43] Vietnam has become a horror symbol of the demonic behavior of the system ruled by men who are no more evil man for man than their most pure-minded critics. It seems we have a repeat of Niebuhr's thesis about "moral man and immoral society."

What is the Christian to do? This is a matter of strategy and tactics. There is no right method. And no one has a blueprint of a new society that is exciting to everyone else. The Christian is not free to do nothing, for to do nothing is already to vote for the status quo. Many Christians will remain perfectly content with the system. There have always been those who favor most what favors them—even at the expense of the least favored. Others will work within the existing institutions of society, trusting in their capacity for self-renewal. A few Christians, like the hermits in the early church, will separate themselves from society. The Christian is free to be a hippie, a fool for Christ's sake. Or he may be a revolutionary, who seeks to replace the present social, political, and economic order with one more humanizing. If this is the case, he has two options: either to attack the system headlong from the outside or to subvert it from the inside. The Christian is not used to thinking of these two tactics as possible for him. Romans 13:1 has made him timid and subservient before all authorities as though they were instituted by God.

Richard Shaull has made a suggestion for a new strategy for

those who wish to take a revolutionary stance. He sees little to be accomplished by moving outside the power structures.[44] Instead, revolutionaries may take a leaf from modern guerrilla warfare and form fighting units or task forces with limited but concrete objectives. They may be "in" but not "of" the structures, applying pressure for change at sensitive points. The idea of a total revolution which wipes the slate clean, leading to an absolutely new beginning, is what Berdyaev once called "a stupid illusion."[45] Instead of *total* revolution Shaull opts for *permanent* revolution.[46] Wendland too rejects the ideology of the absolute revolution.[47] This is not to endorse gradualism or some other euphemism for keeping things pretty much the way they are. A strategy based on guerrilla tactics means that far-reaching revolutionary goals may be held, while striking many short-ranged targets along the way. It is not a question of all or nothing. And Christians may be joined with other revolutionary humanists in these study and action groups. It is hardly to be expected that the bulk of Christian communities will be on the frontiers of revolutionary ferment. At a time, however, when Christians sense the need for new forms of the church relevant to modern needs, it may be that new communities of Christians will emerge at the points where the coming kingdom of God and the revolutionary struggles in the world today meet. Then Christians may learn to pray in earnestness: Thy kingdom come, thy will be done on earth as it is in heaven.

Granted that radical social change is needed, can the Christian advocate violence as a revolutionary technique? Is violence a more immoral form of coercion than the subtle forms in our society which masses of Christians approve by their silence? Violence must be intrinsically abhorrent to the Christian. It can only be justified as a last resort, and even then the rules of the game by which the Christian plays make it better to suffer violence than to inflict it. A Christian who decides for revolutionary change is not an agent of a political party or social group whose dominion he seeks. He is an advance agent of the kingdom of God, acting out in parables the meaning of its coming. The weapons of "blood and iron" are the poorest for this purpose. On the other hand, as the official churches have had little trouble in the past justifying the use of weapons of violence by Christians in wars of national self-interest, hooked as they have been on the ideologies of imperialism or nationalism, it should be no more difficult exonerating the use of violence in revolutionary struggles which aim to build a better tomorrow for all.

Violence is the common denominator in war and revolution. Besides working ahead of time to mitigate the circumstances which make them necessary, Christians must develop a new style of existence *in their midst*. They must come to terms with the factor of violence. Absolute pacifism does not succeed, for in giving the appearance of noninvolvement, it creates the illusion of being free from guilt and responsibility in the matter. It is motivated by a tender moral conscience. An alternative is an eschatological motivation, which places the Christian in the midst of struggle, where he dares to act out already the principles which apply to the new age—seeking justice, freedom, peace, reconciliation, unity—in situations seething with vindictiveness and poisoned by the itch for revenge. The Christian has a "messianic license"[48] to act beyond the norms of the law—especially the law of retaliation and revenge. The powers of the messianic kingdom are at hand. The Christian is free to use them—to support the given structures if they are fluid enough to grow in service to all men, to change them when they block the coming of a more just society, even to overthrow them with force when the controlling powers have become insane and demonic. The martyrdom of Dietrich Bonhoeffer stands as a reminder to modern Christians that the decision to use force may in some situations be the compulsion of love. Indeed, those who live by the sword will die by the sword, but so do a lot of other people—innocent people. To seek the peace of the kingdom by means of the sword is a contradiction. It is a contradiction from which at times there may be no escape. The

pain of this contradiction may then shape itself into a prayer for
the speedy arrival of the kingdom of peace and reconciliation
among men and nations. There will be peace when the Messiah
reigns. "And they shall beat their swords into plowshares, and
their spears into pruning hooks; nation shall not lift up sword
against nation, neither shall they learn war any more."[49] Christians
are to form a peace corps of God's kingdom in the world, an army
of salvation signaling "the way" to a future in which violence will
be no more, and "there shall be an end to death, and to mourning
and crying and pain."[50] That is the final goal of the revolutionary
existence of Christians in the world.

Notes

Introduction. The Horizon of the Future

1. Ernst Bloch, *Das Prinzip Hoffnung* (Frankfurt: Suhrkamp Verlag, 1959), Vol. III, p. 1628.

2. Ernst Benz, *Evolution and Christian Hope*, tr. by Heinz G. Frank (Doubleday & Company, 1966), p. viii.

3. Jürgen Moltmann, *Theology of Hope*, tr. by James W. Leitch (Harper & Row, 1967), p. 16.

4. Gerhard Sauter, *Zukunft und Verheissung: Das Problem der Zukunft in der gegenwärtigen theologischen und philosophischen Diskussion* (Zürich: Zwingli Verlag, 1965).

5. Harvey Cox, "The Death of God and the Future of Theology," *New Theology No. 4*, ed. by Martin E. Marty and Dean G. Peerman (Macmillan Company, 1967), p. 252.

6. Johannes B. Metz, "The Church and the World," *The Word in History, The St. Xavier Symposium*, ed. by T. Patrick Burke (Sheed and Ward, 1966), p. 70.

7. Karl Barth, *The Epistle to the Romans*, tr. by Edwyn C. Hoskyns (Oxford University Press, 1933), p. 314. I have translated this famous quotation differently to remove an error. The German reads: *"Christentum, das nicht ganz und gar und restlos Eschatologie ist, hat mit Christus ganz und gar und restlos nichts zu tun."* Hoskyns' translation reads: "If Christianity be not altogether restless eschatology, there remains in it no relationship whatever with Christ." The German word *restlos* does not mean "restless" but rather "entirely" or "without remainder."

8. This is the heading of the fourth chapter of John A. T. Robinson's *Honest to God,* and the title of a book inspired by it, written by Erik Routley, *The Man for Others* (Oxford University Press, 1964). My critical remark is a general one, directed more at its voguish character than the specific use of it made by Robinson and Routley. Of course, these popular books do nothing to dispel the idea that the ethical picture of the historical Jesus is an arbitrary abstraction apart from the eschatological framework within which Jesus can be presented as "the Man for others" in any supremely significant sense.

9. Ernst Käsemann, "Die Anfänge christlicher Theologie," *Exegetische Versuche und Besinnungen,* Vol. 2 (Gottingen: Vandenhoek & Ruprecht, 1964), p. 100.

10. Käsemann, "Gottesgerechtigkeit bei Paulus," *ibid.,* p. 193: "Paulus ist Apokalyptiker auch als Christ geblieben."

11. See Gerhard Ebeling, "Der Grund christlicher Theologie," *Zeitschrift für Theologie und Kirche,* 58 (1961), 227–34, and Ernest Fuchs, Über die Aufgabe einer christlichen Theologie," *ibid.,* 245–67. See further Käsemann's reply to them in "Zum Thema der urchristlichen Apokalyptik," *ibid.,* 59 (1962), 257–84.

12. Wolfhart Pannenberg, "Hermeneutics and Universal History," *History and Hermeneutic, Journal for Theology and the Church,* Vol. IV, ed. by Robert Funk (Harper & Row, 1967). We will be using the concept of horizon throughout this study. According to one of the dictionary meanings, a *horizon* is the place where the sky meets the earth. In the popular mind, it often conjures up images of the wild blue yonder. Obviously, neither of these meanings would be very helpful. In phenomenological and hermeneutical philosophy *horizon* is a field of vision which includes two sides, one subjective and the other objective. The horizon of the viewer is his subjective standpoint, how he looks out upon the world. The objective pole is the wide range of what comes into view, the outer limits within which anything that appears has its place and meaning. A horizon, accordingly, is not to be thought of as merely subjective or objective, but involves a dynamic situation in which the horizon of the subject attempts to expand continually to overtake the horizon of all that is not yet known. Thus, a horizon is not a closed and fixed situation, neither on the subjective nor on the objective side. This concept is appropriate to a theology of history which asks about the meaning of Jesus Christ as a past-historical event for the present and the future. The Christ-event is an occurrence within the horizon of a particular historical situation that is different from every other one. The hermeneutical task is to understand this event within a new historical situation like our own, without doing violence to the particular character of the two horizons. For other discussions on the concept of horizon, see the following: Bernard Lonergan, "Metaphysics as Horizon," *Collection,* ed. by F. E. Crowe (London: Darton, Longman & Todd, 1967), pp. 213 ff.; Michael Novak, "The Christian and the Atheist," *The Meaning of the Death of God,* ed. by Bernard Murchland (Alfred A. Knopf, 1967), pp. 76 ff., in

which Novak expands on some of Lonergan's ideas; Martin Heidegger, *Being and Time,* tr. by J. Macquarrie and E. Robinson (London: SCM Press, 1962), p. 1, n. 4; H.-G. Gadamer, *Wahrheit und Methode* (Tübingen: J. C. B. Mohr, 1965), pp. 231 ff., 286 ff., 356 ff.; Jürgen Moltmann, *Theology of Hope,* pp. 106, 125, 190–91; Ernst Bloch, *Das Prinzip Hoffnung,* Vol. I, pp. 122–23, 257, 329, 332. Gadamer defines horizon as "something into which we move, and which moves with us. Horizons change for the one who moves" (*op. cit.,* p. 288).

13. A lengthy discussion of the importance of the horizon of the future in the interpretation of universal history can be found in Pannenberg's essay, "Hermeneutics and Universal History," *op. cit.*

14. Rudolph Bultmann, "Is Exegesis Without Presuppositions Possible?" *Existence and Faith,* tr. by Schubert M. Ogden (Meridian Books, 1960), p. 295. Italics mine.

15. *Ibid.* Italics mine.

16. Quoted from Bernard Delfgaauw, *The Young Marx* (Sheed and Ward, 1967), p. 50.

17. See J. B. Metz's article on this idea, "Verantwortung der Hoffnung," *Stimmen der Zeit,* 177, 1966.

18. Matt. 11:12.

19. 1 Pet. 3:15 (KJV).

20. Karl Rahner, "Christianity and the 'New Man,'" *The Christian and the World* (P. J. Kenedy & Sons, 1965), p. 212.

21. Karl Rahner, "Christentum als Religion der absoluten Zukunft," *Christentum und Marxismus—Heute,* ed. by Erich Kellner (Frankfurt: Europa Verlag, 1966), pp. 202–12.

22. Roger Garaudy, "Was uns trennt—was uns verbindet," *ibid.,* p. 319.

23. Karl Menninger, "Hope," *American Journal of Psychiatry* (December, 1959), pp. 481 ff.

24. See William F. Lynch, *Images of Hope* (Helicon Press, 1966).

25. Thomas Aquinas, *Summa Theologica,* Part II (First Part), Q. 40, Art. 3.

26. Teilhard de Chardin, *The Future of Man,* tr. by Norman Denny (Harper & Row, 1964), p. 72.

27. See further refinements of the meaning of *Zukunft* in Jürgen Moltmann's "Antwort auf die Kritik der Theologie der Hoffnung," *Diskussion über die "Theologie der Hoffnung,"* ed. by Wolf-Dieter Marsch (München: Chr. Kaiser Verlag, 1967), p. 210. See also Gerhard Sauter, *Zukunft und Verheissung,* p. 154. He suggests that theology ought to take the etymological difference seriously between *Zu-kunft* as *adventus* and as *futurum.* Emil Brunner had earlier called attention to this important distinction in *Eternal Hope,* tr. by Harold Knight (Westminster Press, 1954), p. 25, n. 1. The idea of the future as *advent,* stemming from the Latin *advenire,* is of Christian origin, born from the expectation of the coming of God's kingdom.

28. See Jürgen Moltmann's "Antwort auf die Kritik der Theologie der Hoffnung," *op. cit.*, pp. 212–13.

29. See Walter Nigg, *Das ewige Reich, Geschichte einer Hoffnung* (München: Siebenstern Taschenbuch Verlag, 1967).

30. H. Richard Niebuhr, *The Kingdom of God in America* (Harper & Row, 1937).

31. *Ibid.*, p. 193.

32. Walter Rauschenbusch, *A Theology for the Social Gospel* (Abingdon Press, 1945), p. 128.

33. *Ibid.*, p. 135.

34. *Ibid.*, p. 277.

35. Harvey Cox, *The Secular City* (Macmillan Company, 1965), p. 80.

Chapter I. The Phenomenon of Hope – Man

1. Immanuel Kant, *Critique of Pure Reason* (London: J. M. Dent & Sons, 1934), p. 457.

2. Bloch, *Das Prinzip Hoffnung*, Vol. III, p. 1404.

3. Paul Ricoeur, *The Symbolism of Evil*, tr. by Emerson Buchanan (Harper & Row, 1967), p. 348.

4. John Macquarrie, *Principles of Christian Theology* (Charles Scribner's Sons, 1966), pp. 48 ff.

5. Karl Rahner, "Theology and Anthropology," *The Word in History*, ed. by T. P. Burke (Sheed and Ward, 1966), pp. 2 ff.

6. We have two volumes in English, *The Symbolism of Evil*, already cited, and *Fallible Man* (Henry Regnery Company, 1966).

7. See Gabriel Marcel, *Homo Viator: Introduction to a Metaphysic of Hope*, tr. by Emma Craufurd (Henry Regnery Company, 1951), pp. 30 ff.

8. See Ricoeur, *The Symbolism of Evil*, pp. 50–53.

9. J. Moltmann responds to a charge made by Walter Künneth that the theology of both Pannenberg and himself is lacking a satanology, in *Diskussion über die "Theologie der Hoffnung,"* p. 230, n. 28.

10. Mircea Eliade, *Cosmos and History: The Myth of the Eternal Return*, tr. by Willard R. Trask (Harper & Row, 1959).

11. We have adopted Tillich's insight and phraseology: "The principle of all utopias is the *negation of the negative"* ("Die Politische Bedeutung der Utopie im Leben der Völker"), *Der Widerstreit von Raum und Zeit, Gesammelte Werke* (Stuttgart: Evangelisches Verlagswerk, 1963), Vol. VI, p. 186.

12. Søren Kierkegaard, *The Concept of Dread*, tr. by Walter Lowrie (Princeton University Press, 1944).

13. Rom. 4:18 (NEB).

14. Gen. 12:1–2. Unless otherwise indicated, Scripture quotations are from the Revised Standard Version.

15. Bloch, *Das Prinzip Hoffnung*, Vol. III, p. 1457.

16. *Ibid.,* p. 1458.

17. See "A Concordance of Hope," in *The Meaning of Hope,* by C. F. D. Moule (Fortress Press, 1963), pp. 58–71.

18. "Hope," by Rudolf Bultmann and Karl Rengstorf, *Bible Key Words,* from Gerhard Kittel's *Theologisches Wörterbuch zum Neuen Testament* (London: Adam Charles Black, 1963), p. 9.

19. *Ibid.,* p. 11.

20. Ps. 71:5.

21. Quoted by Gerhard Sauter, *Zukunft und Verheissung,* p. 60, n. 38.

22. Moltmann, *Theology of Hope,* p. 126.

23. Jeremiah 29:11: "For I know the plans I have for you, says the Lord, plans for welfare and not for evil, to give you a future and a hope."

24. Exod. 20:5 and Deut. 5:9.

25. See Chapter II, "The Power of the Future," Sections 3 and 4.

26. Dietrich Bonhoeffer, *Letters and Papers from Prison,* tr. by Reginald H. Fuller (Macmillan Company, 1953), p. 163.

27. *Ibid.,* p. 164.

28. Karl Barth, *Church Dogmatics,* I, 2, under the sections entitled "Religion as Unbelief" and "The True Religion."

29. Bonhoeffer, *Letters and Papers from Prison,* p. 230.

30. *Ibid.,* p. 205.

31. *Ibid.,* p. 169.

32. This phrase is borrowed from the title of Robert W. Jenson's book *A Religion Against Itself* (John Knox Press, 1967), whose eschatological orientation accounts for many similarities with my own viewpoint.

33. Quoted by Ingo Hermann, "Total Humanism," *Is God Dead? Concilium,* Vol. 16, p. 161. See also Roger Garaudy, *From Anathema to Dialogue,* tr. by Luke O'Neill (Herder and Herder, 1966).

34. Bloch, *Das Prinzip Hoffnung,* Vol. III, p. 1404.

35. Luke 24:21.

36. Acts 26:6–8.

37. Bonhoeffer, *Letters and Papers from Prison,* p. 230.

Chapter II. The Power of the Future – God

1. See *supra,* p. 37.

2. It is an open question for me how to take the measure of John B. Cobb's book *A Christian Natural Theology* (Westminster Press, 1965), with respect to the task of systematic theology today. What is not yet clear to me is the character and the content of the theology in the light of which Cobb's own construction of a Whiteheadian natural theology might be called "Christian." What makes it "Christian"? It might even seem that this "Christian natural theology" could stand by itself, without need of any supplementation, and therefore be taken, contrary to Cobb's intention, as a substitute for a genuinely

Christian theology based on the revelatory history of God in the person of Jesus of Nazareth. Can it not be said of Whitehead as surely as of Heidegger that what we have is as much a "secularized Christian theology" as a "Christian natural theology"? Is the Whiteheadian scheme, furthermore, one in which the *eschatological* dimension of reality as history and the future-oriented character of man as a hoping creature can adequately be brought to expression? In principle I agree with the need for something that could be called "a Christian natural theology," though the phrase itself does not enchant me; however, I am not yet in fact able to recognize that what Cobb has found in Whitehead is what we need.

3. Rom. 4:17.

4. John 14:9 (KJV).

5. Moltmann, *Theology of Hope,* p. 304.

6. Pannenberg, "Der Gott der Hoffnung," *Grundfragen systematischer Theologie* (Göttingen: Vandenhoek und Ruprecht, 1967), p. 397.

7. In my book *History and Hermeneutics,* Chapter VII, "Eschatology and History," pp. 160–79.

8. Moltmann, *Diskussion über die "Theologie der Hoffnung,"* p. 209.

9. Luke 9:62.

10. Matt. 12:39–40; Luke 11:29.

11. Rom. 8:11.

12. Rom. 4:17.

13. 1 Thess. 4:13.

14. Rom. 11:15.

15. Rom. 4:24.

16. See 1 Thess. 1:10.

17. See 1 Cor. 15:17.

18. Paul Tillich, *Systematic Theology* (University of Chicago Press, 1957), Vol. II, pp. 156–57. The idea of "restitution" does not do justice to the event of the resurrection as something utterly novel. The resurrection is not a restoration or restitution to a previous condition of life. The prefix *re-* in resurrection to be sure, necessarily entails an element of "restoration" or "restitution," namely, attaining a condition of life *again.* Yet, the resurrection event is a going forward to a *new* condition of life, a final exodus out of a death and separation from God, into a permanent union with God in the fullness of his glory. Tillich's symbol of "restitution" is laden with the Hellenistic idea of final salvation as a *restitutio in integrum.* See J. Moltmann's discussion of the effects of the idea of restitution in Christian theology in "Die Kategorie *Novum* in der christlichen Theologie," *Ernst Bloch zu ehren,* ed. by Siegfried Unseld (Frankfurt: Suhrkamp Verlag, 1965), pp. 251–55.

19. Heb. 11:1.

20. Rom. 8:25.

21. Bloch, *Das Prinzip Hoffnung,* Vol. III, p. 1301.

22. *Ibid.,* pp. 1289 f.
23. 1 Cor. 15:54.
24. 1 Pet. 1:3.
25. 1 Cor. 15:28.

Chapter III. The Presence of the Future – Jesus

1. Quoted by Ulrich Asendorf, *Eschatologie bei Luther* (Göttingen: Vandenhoek & Ruprecht, 1967), p. 13.
2. 1 Cor. 2:2.
3. Rom. 8:24.
4. I refer not only to Bultmann but also to Tillich and Barth. In what sense does it make sense to speak of the unity of cross and resurrection? Is it meant both ontically and noetically? Is it not equally important to stress the inherent contradiction between cross and resurrection, so that the resurrection is proclaimed as "the negation of negativity," as the death of death itself?
5. See W. Pannenberg, *Jesus—God and Man,* tr. by Lewis L. Wilkins and Duane A. Priebe (Westminster Press, 1968), p. 246.
6. Willi Marxsen, *Anfangsprobleme der Christologie* (Gütersloher Verlagshaus Gerd Mohn, 1960), pp. 22 f.
7. Bertolt Brecht's epilogue to *The Good Person of Szechwan* opens up the issue. "Should men be better? Should the world be changed? Or just the gods? Or ought there to be none?" He is expressing the intolerableness of accepting things just the way they are. "There must be happy endings, must, must, must!" The eschatological christology of the New Testament asserts the actuality of a possibility of a "happy ending" under the sign of promise, held fast by hope toward the future of God's fulfilling city of peace and righteousness.
8. Rev. 21:4.
9. See Moltmann's discussion, *Theology of Hope,* p. 159.
10. See Ernst Käsemann's stirring address on this theme, delivered at the Kirchentag in Hannover, 1967. The sermon-address is entitled "Die Gegenwart des Gekreuzigten," in *Christus unter uns* (Stuttgart: Kreuz-Verlag, 1967), p. 6.
11. Here lies, I think, the basic deficiency in the otherwise attractive view of the atonement presented by Gustaf Aulèn in his little classic, *Christus Victor.*
12. See Dorothee Soelle, *Christ the Representative: An Essay in Theology after the "Death of God,"* tr. by David Lewis (Fortress Press, 1967). She writes, "He is a representative, not a replacement" (p. 104), which contains the kernel of the idea we are presenting here. Prior to her reflections on this christological motif, Pannenberg had already developed it as a fundamental concept in his christology. See his section on "Jesus as Representative of Men before God," *Jesus—God and Man,* pp. 195–207.
13. Heb. 13:12.
14. Especially Acts 2:36. "Let all the house of Israel therefore know as-

suredly that God has made him both Lord and Christ, this Jesus whom you crucified."

15. The echoes here of Kazoh Kitamori's *Theology of the Pain of God* (John Knox Press, 1965) are unmistakable, and I gratefully acknowledge an affinity with its way of thinking of a "God in pain."

16. Soelle, *Christ the Representative*, p. 104.

17. *Ibid.*, p. 132.

18. See Bonhoeffer's enigmatic statement, "The only way to be honest is to recognize that we have to live in the world *etsi deus non daretur.*" This is not all that Bonhoeffer said, however. He went on to say, "Before God and with him we live without God." *Letters and Papers from Prison*, p. 219. Bonhoeffer's statements throughout are dialectically phrased. One can reach the position of the latter-day left-wing Bonhoefferians only by flattening out the dialectic and taking the one side by itself.

19. Niebuhr, *The Kingdom of God in America*, p. 193.

20. Ernst Käsemann, "God's Righteousness in Paul," *The Bultmann School of Biblical Interpretations: New Directions?* Vol. I of *Journal for Theology and the Church* (Harper Torchbooks, 1965), p. 104.

21. Rom. 4:25.

22. Matt. 6:33 (KJV).

23. Käsemann, "God Righteousness in Paul," *op. cit.*, pp. 102 f.

24. *Ibid.*, p. 104.

25. P. Tillich's expression in his lecture on Luther, in "The Recovery of the Prophetic Tradition in the Reformation," published in German translation in *Gesammelte Werke*, VII.

26. The idea of God's present as "anonymous demand" is more fully expounded by Gustaf Wingren, *Creation and Law*, tr. by Ross Mackenzie (Muhlenberg Press, 1961), pp. 57 ff.

27. *Proceedings of the Fourth Assembly of the LWF, Helsinki, 1963* (Berlin: Lutherisches Verlagshaus, 1965), p. 426.

28. For evidence to the contrary, see Wilhelm Dantine, "Rechtfertigung und Gottesgerechtigkeit," *Verkündigung und Forschung, Beihefte zu "Evangelische Theologie"* (1966), 11. Jahrgang, Heft 2, pp. 68 ff. Better yet is his major work, *Die Gerechtmachung des Gottlosen* (München: Chr. Kaiser Verlag, 1959).

29. I have tried to trace some of the distortions of the doctrine of justification in the history of Protestant Christianity in "The Correlation of Justification and Faith in Evangelical Dogmatics," *The New Community in Christ*, ed. by J. Burtness and J. Kildahl (Augsburg Publishing House, 1963).

30. See Gerhard Gloege, *Gnade für die Welt: Kritik und Krise des Luthertums* (Göttingen: Vandenhoek & Ruprecht, 1964).

31. See Krister Stendahl, "The Apostle Paul and the Introspective Conscience

of the West," *The Harvard Theological Review,* LVI: 3 (July, 1963), 199–216.

32. Käsemann, "God's Righteousness in Paul," *op. cit.,* p. 109. In this article Käsemann is criticizing the existentialist tendency to reduce Paul's message to the experience of the individual person.

33. Gal. 5:5.

34. Phil. 3:12–13.

35. Peter Stuhlmacher, "Erwägungen zum Problem von Gegenwart und Zukunft in der paulinischen Eschatologie," *Zeitschrift für Theologie und Kirche* (1964), 64, Heft 4, p. 449. "Die paulinische Eschatologie ist eine proleptische und darin christologische Eschatologie."

36. Peter Stuhlmacher, *Gerechtigkeit Gottes bei Paulus* (Göttingen: Vandenhoek & Ruprecht, 1964); Käsemann, "God's Righteousness in Paul," *op. cit.*

37. *Ibid.,* p. 101.

38. 2 Pet. 3:13.

39. Rom. 8:18 (Phillips).

40. Tillich, *Systematic Theology,* Vol. III, p. 291.

41. Gerhard Sauter, *Zukunft und Verheissung,* p. 174. See also pp. 149 ff., 162 ff., 292, 307.

42. For example, Oscar Cullmann, *Christ and Time,* tr. by Floyd V. Filson (Westminster Press, 1950).

43. Romans 4:17.

44. W. Pannenberg, "Analogie und Doxologie," *Grundfragen systematischer Theologie,* p. 201.

45. For example, see John 1:1–3; Heb. 1:2–3; Eph. 1:3–14; Phil. 2:5–11; Col. 1:15–20; cf. also 1 Cor. 8:6.

46. Otto A. Dilschneider, *Christus Pantokrator: Vom Kolosserbrief zur Ökumene* (Berlin: Vogt, 1962).

47. Tillich, *Systematic Theology,* Vol. III, p. 293.

48. Joel 2:28–32; Acts 2:16–21.

49. Luke 4:17 ff.

50. 2 Cor. 3:17.

51. Rom. 8:14.

52. John 20:21–22.

53. Tillich, *Systematic Theology,* Vol. III, p. 291.

54. See W. Pannenberg, "Theology and the Kingdom of God," *Una Sancta,* 24, 2, pp. 17–18; also *Jesus—God and Man,* p. 181; "Der Gott der Hoffnung," *Grundfragen systematischer Theologie,* pp. 397–98; Moltmann, *Diskussion über die "Theologie der Hoffnung,"* pp. 221–22; Walter Künneth, *The Theology of the Resurrection,* tr. by James W. Leitch (Concordia Publishing House, 1965), p. 194.

Chapter IV. The Prolepsis of a New World – Church

1. Wolfhart Pannenberg's article, "The Kingdom of God and the Church," *Una Sancta,* 24 (Christmas, 1967), 4, offers a sketch of interlocking relations among the kingdom of God, the church, and the world. This chapter is following up many of the clues which I have received from it.

2. The Augsburg Confession, Art. VII.

3. On church-centered thinking, see J. C. Hoekendijk, *The Church Inside Out,* tr. by Isaac C. Rottenberg (Westminster Press, 1966), the entirety of which is a polemic against the centripetal tendencies in the church's traditional thought forms and institutions.

4. Gustave Weigel, "Catholic Eccesiology in Our Time," *Christianity Divided* (Sheed and Ward, 1961), pp. 179–80.

5. *Ibid.,* p. 177.

6. See the articles by Y. Congar, E. Schillebeeckx, and R. Schnackenburg in *The Church and Mankind,* Vol. 1 of *Concilium* (Paulist Press, 1965).

7. See my article, "The New Social Gospel Movement," *Dialog* (Spring, 1966), Vol. 5, p. 133.

8. Acts 17:6.

9. Heb. 13:14.

10. Jas. 1:18; Rom. 8:23.

11. 1 Cor. 15:20, 23; Col. 1:18.

12. 2 Cor. 5:17 (NEB).

13. See the discussion by Karl Rahner, "The Theology of the Symbol," *Theological Investigations,* tr. by Kevin Smyth (Helicon Press, 1966), Vol. IV, pp. 221 ff.

14. Paul Tillich, "Nature and Sacrament," *The Protestant Era* (University of Chicago Press, 1948), pp. 94 ff.

15. Kornelis H. Miskotte's *When the Gods Are Silent,* tr. by John W. Doberstein (London: Collins, 1967), interprets the Old Testament as full of prolepses of the new world, of the fullness of the future, which dawns in the history of Christ.

16. 1 Cor. 11:26.

17. Albert Schweitzer, *The Mysticism of Paul the Apostle* (Adam and Charles Black, 1931), p. 251.

18. Mark 14:25; see also Luke 22:18.

19. Quoted from a Paschal hymn in the Eastern Orthodox tradition, Alexander Schmemann, *For the Life of the World* (National Student Christian Federation, 1963), p. 40.

20. See Roy A. Harrisville's *The Concept of Newness in the New Testament* (Augsburg Publishing House, 1960), esp. pp. 84–85. His thesis is that the newness which the gospel proclaims is placed within the horizon of the eschatological future, but that now already, on account of Christ, it is possible to

live from the power of that future. "In this condition it is still possible for him to sin, and indeed, he does sin, *but he need not*" (pp. 85 f.). The necessity of sin no longer has the same old grip on a person's will. One could say that the Christian does continue to sin, but he enjoys it less.

21. Phil. 3:12–14.

22. Rom. 6:4.

23. Leslie Dewart, *The Future of Belief* (Herder & Herder, 1966), pp. 203–4.

24. See, for examples, Pss. 6:3; 13:1–2; 35:17; 74:10; 79:5; 89:46; 90:13; Isa. 6:11; Jer. 12:4; Hab. 1:2; Zech. 1:12; Rev. 6:10.

25. I have dealt with this problem at greater length in an article, "The Reunited Church of the Future," *Journal of Ecumenical Studies* (Autumn, 1967).

26. The operation was a marvelous success; but unfortunately the patient died.

27. See Pannenberg, "The Kingdom of God and the Church," *op. cit.,* pp. 22 ff.

28. Dewart, *The Future of Belief,* pp. 127–28. The reviews of Dewart's book, collected in *The Future of Belief Debate,* ed. by Gregory Baum (Herder & Herder, 1967), whether pro or con, do not emphasize clearly enough that the real point of the book is not so much the negative one of *de-Hellenization* as it is the positive one of *reeschatologization.* The Hellenization of Christian belief once effected a deeschatologization, as the price to pay for the universalization of the Christian truth in the realm of Hellenistic metaphysics. Perhaps Dewart himself did not make clear enough that the pressure behind de-Hellenization is not merely the need for modernization, but is one arising out of the eschatological dimension of the history of Christ. The ambiguity in the book stems, I think, from a deficient eschatology, which makes his program of modernization (theism in a world come of age) inadequately grounded in the past-historical prolepsis of the eschatological future. Therefore the criterion of truth seems to be at the mercy of the prevailing spirit of the age.

29. See Wolfhart Pannenberg's discussion of syncretism in "Erwägungen zu einer Theologie der Religionsgeschichte," *Grundfragen systematischer Theologie,* pp. 269 ff.

30. Quoted from J. C. Hoekendijk, *Kirche und Volk in der deutschen Missionswissenschaft* (München: Chr. Kaiser Verlag, 1967), p. 19.

31. Martin Kähler, "Die Mission; ist sie ein unentbehrlicher Zug am Christentume?" *Dogmatische Zeitfragen,* II (Leipzig: A. Deichert'sche Verlagsbuchhandlung Nachf., 1908), p. 347.

Chapter V. The Politics of Hope – Society

1. Tillich, "Storms of Our Times," *The Protestant Era.*

2. The two strongest theological voices were Heinz-Dietrich Wendland of Münster, Germany, and Richard Shaull of Princeton, New Jersey. The theological essays in the preparatory volume, *Christian Social Ethics in a Changing*

World, ed. by John Bennett (Association Press, 1966), lagged conceptually far behind the revolutionary phenomena that the nontheologians kept pressing to the front at the Geneva conference.

3. Harvey Cox, *The Secular City,* p. 107.

4. Hannah Arendt, *On Revolution* (Viking Press, 1963), p. 8.

5. See Karl Rahner, "Über die Einheit von Nächsten—und Gottesliebe," *Schriften zur Theologie* (Zürich: Benziger Verlag Einsideln, 1965), Vol. VI, pp. 277–300.

6. Arend Th. van Leeuwen, *Christianity in World History,* tr. by H. H. Hoskins (Charles Scribner's Sons, 1964), pp. 332, 344, and in general the whole of Chapter VI, "The Revolutionary West."

7. "Augustine replaced the early expectation of the end of time by an ecclesiastical positivism which equates the visible Catholic Church with the Kingdom of God." Ernst Benz, *Evolution and Christian Hope,* p. 26.

8. Heinrich Bornkamm, *Luther's Doctrine of the Two Kingdoms,* tr. by Karl Hertz (Fortress Press, 1966), p. 20.

9. William H. Lazareth, "Luther's 'Two Kingdoms' Ethic Reconsidered," *Christian Social Ethics in a Changing World,"* p. 121.

10. Ulrich Asendorf, *Eschatologie bei Luther* (Göttingen: Vandenhoek und Ruprecht, 1967). See esp. III, 2, "Die Regimentenlehre im Zusammenhang der Eschatologie," pp. 248–80. Asendorf demonstrates that the key to understanding Luther's two-kingdom doctrine is his eschatology. Eschatology is the basis for the unity of the two kingdoms. The charge that the weakness in Luther's doctrine is its noneschatological structure is, Asendorf says, a "grotesque misunderstanding" (p. 250). Asendorf does not sufficiently see, however, that the question to be addressed to Luther's two-kingdom doctrine is not only *whether* eschatology governs Luther's conception but *what kind of* eschatology does so. I fail to find in his treatment of Luther the eschatological basis for anything but a conservative stance of the Christian or of the church in the world. God manages the secular realm with his left hand. To do something with one's left hand connotes doing it in a clumsy and halfhearted way. Why should theology assume that God is the archconservative in the political and social realm?

11. Paul Tillich, *A History of Christian Thought,* ed. by Carl E. Braaten (Harper and Row, 1968), p. 255.

12. The Augsburg Confession, Article XVI on "Civil Government," and Luther's "Temporal Authority: To What Extent It Should Be Obeyed," *Luther's Works,* ed. by Walter Brandt (Muhlenberg Press, 1962), American edition, Vol. 45.

13. How this has happened generally in the Lutheran tradition is clearly exhibited in Einar Billing's little work *Our Calling.* He collapses the entire biblical theology of the kingdom of God into the forgiveness of sins. The concept of the forgiveness of sins is hardly adequate to encompass an understanding of the social relations of our time. Billing is afraid of making the

kingdom of God and the forgiveness of sins two foci in an ellipse, so he sub-
sumes the kingdom of God motif under the forgiveness of sins. But why not
then the other way around, if only one principle there must be? ". . . the
forgiveness of sins means ultimately nothing less than the totality of all the
ways God has taken in history to build his kingdom. The kingdom of God is
nothing else than the actualization of the forgiveness of sins." *Our Calling*
(Fortress Press, 1965), p. 16. Italics mine.

14. The Augsburg Confession, Article XVI. Tappert edition, pp. 37 f.

15. Tillich, *Systematic Theology,* Vol. III, p. 355.

16. See Oscar Cullmann, "The Kingship of Christ and the Church in the
New Testament," *The Early Church,* ed. by A. J. B. Higgins (Westminster
Press, 1956), pp. 105 ff.

17. Matt. 11:5. (Author's translation).

18. Revolutionaries are almost always recruitable only among the victims of
social injustice. In writing of the French Revolution, Hannah Arendt observes
that those who burst into the streets of Paris were "actually the multitude of
the poor and the downtrodden, whom every century before had hidden in
darkness and shame." *On Revolution,* p. 41.

19. "Institutional separation" and "functional interaction" are key formulae
in the revised version of the two-kingdom doctrine published by the Board
of Social Ministry of the Lutheran Church in America, entitled *Church and
State: A Lutheran Perspective.* Unfortunately, both of the chapters on "Biblical
Witness" and "Ethical Guidelines" are completely void of the eschatological
perspective which has recently been demonstrated in New Testament studies as
fundamental to the gospel and the church's understanding of its life in the
world, as well as of the world's own meaning and future.

20. Arendt, *On Revolution,* p. 15.

21. Garaudy, *From Anathema to Dialogue,* p. 56.

22. Heinz-Dietrich Wendland, "Church and Revolution," *The Ecumenical
Review,* XVIII (1966), 444.

23. Tillich, "Historical and Nonhistorical Interpretations of History," *The
Protestant Era,* p. 24.

24. See Ernst Benz, *Ecclesia Spiritualis* (Stuttgart: W. Kohlhammer Verlag,
1964). This is a comprehensive treatment of the influence of Joachim of
Fiore's idea of the church and theology of history on the later Franciscan
radicals. See also Benz's chapter on Joachim in *Evolution and Christian Hope.*

25. John 14:12.

26. See the most recent study by Eric Gritsch, *Prophet Without a Church*
(Fortress Press, 1967).

27. Benz, *Evolution and Christian Hope,* p. 56.

28. See, for example, Wilhelm Mühlmann, *Chiliasmus und Nativismus:
Studien zur Psychologie, Soziologie und historischen Kasuistik der Umsturzbewe-
gungen* (Berlin, 1961).

29. Eugen Rosenstock-Huessy, *The Christian Future* (Charles Scribner's Sons, 1946), p. 168.

30. See Herbert Marcuse's attack on "one-dimensionalism" in his book, *One-Dimensional Man* (Beacon Press, 1964).

31. This judgment does not preclude the possibility of reinterpreting natural-law theory in a more dynamic way. Michael Novak writes about a new type of natural-law theory, held by some Catholic philosophers, e.g., Bernard Lonergan, who "contends that natural law is not immutable and 'out there' but is developing and intrinsic to man's active and inventive intelligence. There are unchanging principles of natural law only in the sense in which *operations of intelligence* are principles, not in the sense in which *propositions,* precepts, or premises are principles." Michael Novak, "Secular Style and Natural Law," *The Secular City Debate,* ed. by Daniel Callahan (Macmillan Company, 1966), pp. 81–82.

32. Arendt, *On Revolution,* p. 234.

33. *Ibid.,* p. 284.

34. *Ibid.*

35. Richard Shaull, "Revolution: Heritage and Contemporary Option," *Containment and Change,* coauthored with Carl Oglesby (Macmillan Company, 1967), p. 190.

36. Van Leeuwen, *Christianity in World History,* p. 435.

37. Cox, *The Secular City,* p. 120.

38. *Ibid.,* p. 119.

39. Carl Oglesby, "Vietnamese Crucible," *Containment and Change,* p. 147.

40. *Ibid.,* p. 148.

41. *Ibid.,* p. 151.

42. *Ibid.,* pp. 152–54.

43. Richard Shaull, *Containment and Change,* p. 189.

44. *Ibid.,* p. 196.

45. Nicolas Berdyaev, *Slavery and Freedom* (London: Geoffrey Bles: The Centenary Press, 1944). "Revolution supposes at first that it is possible to annihilate the past so that nothing remains of it, *du passé faisons la table rase*—a stupid illusion" (p. 197).

46. Shaull, *Containment and Change,* p. 238.

47. Heinz-Dietrich Wendland, "The Church and Revolution," *Christian Social Ethics in a Changing World,* p. 451.

48. This idea has been advanced by Krister Stendahl in an unpublished paper entitled "Messianic License," written in 1962. He states: "The messianic license would mean that Jesus gave his disciples the permission, the license to act in a way which undercuts the very structure on which society is built. . . . The Sermon on the Mount is actually a rebellious manifesto which gives to the disciples of Christ the right to break the law in the name of Christ.

But it is important to remember that it is subversive, and that the disciples must be prepared to pay the price for such action. So it was then and so it may be now."

49. Isa. 2:4; also Mic. 4:3.
50. Rev. 21:4 (NEB).

Index
of Names

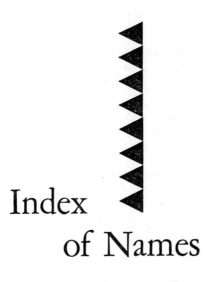

Designed by Robert Freese
Set in Garamond
Composed and printed by York Composition Co., Inc.
Bound by The Haddon Craftsmen, Inc.
HARPER & ROW, PUBLISHERS, INCORPORATED

69 70 71 72 73 8 7 6 5 4 3 2 1